THE

Grilled Cheese Madonna

and 99 Other of the Weirdest, Wackiest,

Most Famous eBay Auctions Ever

Broadway Books

NEW YORK

Christopher Cihlar

THE

Grilled Cheese Madonna
and 99 Other of the Weirdest, Wackiest,
Most Famous eBay Auctions Ever

BROADWAY

PUBLISHED BY BROADWAY BOOKS

Copyright © 2006 by Christopher Cihlar

Published in the United States by Broadway Books, an imprint of The Doubleday Broadway Publishing Group, a division of Random House, Inc., New York.

www.broadwaybooks.com

BROADWAY BOOKS and its logo, a letter B bisected on the diagonal, are trademarks of Random House, Inc.

Book design by Elizabeth Rendfleisch

Library of Congress Cataloging-in-Publication Data
Cihlar, Christopher.
    The grilled cheese madonna and 99 other of the weirdest, wackiest, most famous eBay auctions ever / by Christopher Cihlar.
        p.   cm.
        1. eBay (Firm)—Case studies. 2. Internet auctions—Case studies.
3. Internet marketing—Case studies. I. Title: Weirdest, wackiest, most famous eBay auctions ever. II. eBay (Firm) III. Title.
HF5478.C54 2006
381'.177—dc22   2005054276

ISBN-13: 978-0-7679-2374-3
ISBN-10: 0-7679-2374-X

PRINTED IN THE UNITED STATES OF AMERICA

10 9 8 7 6 5 4 3 2 1

First Edition

For **Kalinka** *and* **Shay**

CONTENTS

Contents

Contents

THE

Grilled Cheese Madonna

and 99 Other of the Weirdest, Wackiest, Most Famous eBay Auctions Ever

Introduction

Over the years eBay has become one of the most successful
Internet-based businesses, and every day millions of
people from around the world buy and sell almost
everything imaginable via the online auction site. Occasionally one of these auctions captures the attention of the
general public, reaps financial windfalls for owners of
seemingly worthless items, and makes some sellers household names. What American does not know of whom you
speak when you say, "The Wedding Dress Guy"? Now,
through careful study of the ten lessons presented on the
pages that follow, you too have the opportunity to learn
how to achieve fame and fortune by hosting your own
eBay sale!

Have you always wanted to appear next to Jay Leno on

The Tonight Show but have thus far failed to attract his attention? Then this book is for you. From the "Ghost in a Jar" auction that recorded more than a million page views (number of times the auction was seen by an eBay user), to the seller who offered the raft he claimed had carried Elian Gonzalez to the United States, to the attempted sale of a human kidney—this book chronicles the one hundred most famous eBay listings and is peppered with helpful hints about how you can best go about making your own auction a vehicle for fame and fortune.

The auctions presented in *The Grilled Cheese Madonna* are sometimes bizarre, sometimes politically motivated, but all were, for some reason or another, newsworthy. For the first time ever, the most famous eBay auctions and the stories behind them are presented in one place.

How to Sell Yourself

The first thing any career counselor or self-help guru will tell you is that the key to success in life is learning how to sell yourself. Some of the authors of the most noteworthy and notorious eBay auctions took that advice literally. From the man who put his own kidney up for sale to the woman who auctioned off her virginity, one of the most established strategies for attracting significant media attention to an auction is to try to sell something you were born with.

The auctions presented in this section highlight some of the more creative ways people have sought to market pieces of themselves. Is there a vital organ you are not using that someone else might find essential? Have you been looking for the opportunity to part with your precious virginity? Are you willing to part with your soul, or would you prefer simply to walk around town with an advertisement plastered to your forehead? Get creative! The auctions described on the following pages are meant to inspire, and you need not be limited by what has already been done.

A word of caution, though: eBay often frowns upon these types of sales. The company has established a set of regulations that prohibit selling many of your most valuable assets. You should also check the laws that are applicable to your particular situation, as several of the auctions depicted in this section are not only against eBay policy, but also illegal.

Still, even if your auction is against formal eBay policy, take heart. It may generate sufficient publicity so that should eBay take down your listing, you will be able to continue the auction outside of eBay's domain, as a couple of more ambitious sellers discussed in this lesson did. Remember, millions of items are listed for sale on eBay every week. If you hope to have success in this competitive arena, you need to be willing to do what the other guy is not.

YOUR AD GOES HERE: PART I

Advertisers are always looking for new and innovative places to market their products. While television, radio, and print ads are the most common, you can find advertisements almost anywhere you look. From the subway to the elevator to the golf course, companies seek out previously untapped venues where they can place an ad that will garner as much attention as possible. In early 2005, eBay helped one entrepreneurial young man open a previously untapped market: the human forehead.

Twenty-year-old college student Andrew Fischer from Omaha, Nebraska, offered the highest bidder in eBay auction number 5950507719 the opportunity to have their nonpermanent logo or brand name tattooed to his forehead for thirty days. According to the auction's description, this "Average Joe" would display the winning bidder's advertisement in all types of venues that the "Average Joe" frequented in his hometown of 600,000. Fischer's offer turned up in news stories published far from his native Omaha. The auction received more than 300,000 hits and recorded a final sale price of $30,000.

In a seemingly unfortunate occurrence, the winning bidder never contacted the seller and Fischer was forced to resubmit the auction with controls put in place to limit who could bid. Attention the second time around was just as intense and, by the time the auction ended, 45 bids had pushed the final sale price to $37,375. The winner was Christian de Rivel, CEO of SnoreStop, an oral spray designed to help alleviate snoring.

De Rivel's money seems to have been well spent. The story was picked up by media outlets all over the world, and, according to de Rivel, sales through his Web site went up fivefold in the days after the auction ended. Numerous imitators cropped up, including both a man and a woman who offered to permanently tattoo the winning bidder's brand onto their foreheads. Unfortunately for these would-be advertisers, none enjoyed the same monetary success as Fischer.

YOUR AD GOES HERE: PART II

Amber Rainey was in the third trimester of her pregnancy when Andrew Fischer was receiving international news coverage for auctioning off his forehead. After seeing the astronomical price the auction commanded, she looked at her growing belly and realized she had far more advertising space there than Andrew Fischer had on his forehead. Thus auction 3869933040 was conceived.

Titled "Advertising Space Available ON MY PREGNANT BELLY!" Rainey's auction went live on January 25, 2005. According to the description of the auction, the seller's baby was due March 21, and, as she put it, "People can't help but look at a pregnant woman's bump." The mother-to-be said she would not advertise anything she deemed to be offensive or put anything on her belly that would harm her or her unborn child. But, other than that, she would allow potential buyers the artistic freedom to create the advertisement of their choosing.

The auction, ending on February 5 after a one-week stint on eBay, attracted national news coverage, more than 50,000 visits, 97 bids, and a final sale price of $4,050. The winning bidder was GoldenPalace.com, an online casino notorious for its outlandish eBay buys. The casino immediately saw its advertising dollars pay huge dividends when Rainey scored an appearance on NBC's *Today* show. She has also been covered on the national CBS *Evening*

News as well as appeared on numerous local television stations and in print in newspapers, magazines, and on Internet sites around the world. Considering that an advertisement on either CBS's *Evening News* or the *Today* show would cost many times what GoldenPalace.com paid for space on Amber's belly, the arrangement seems to have paid off nicely.

THE HUMAN KIDNEY: WHO NEEDS TWO?

Posted by a seller from Sunrise, Florida, the ad read simply:

> "Fully functional kidney for sale. You can choose either kidney. Buyer pays all transplant and medical costs. Of course only one for sale, as I need the other one to live. Serious bids only."

What ensued was a flood of attention and debate from around the world.

The auction began with an opening bid of $25,000. By the time eBay intervened and pulled the auction, the asking price had reached $5.7 million. Steve Westley, eBay's vice president of marketing at the time, stated, "EBay has zero tolerance for illegal items on this site. We have a very clear policy against this."

Indeed, selling one's kidney or, for that matter, any body part is against federal law in the United States and punishable by up to five years in prison and/or a $50,000 fine. Since 1984, when the U.S. Congress passed the National Organ Transplant Act, organ donation has been set up as a gift program.

On September 2, 1999, immediately following the canceling of the proffered item by eBay, a second seller, this one from Bel Air, Maryland, added fuel to the fire by trying to circumvent federal law when he offered his own kidney for sale to benefit a charity, stating, "Will donate perfect healthy kidney for a reciprocal donation of 2.5 million dollars to a charity of my choice." This sale was summarily shut down by eBay.

While there is no way to know whether these sale or purchase offers were authentic, the idea of putting body parts up for sale generated a significant amount of ethical debate by academics, news organizations, and the general public. In the years since these two kidneys first attracted the media's spotlight, eBay has also stopped the auctions of livers, an entire cadaver, sperm, and human eggs. Selling sperm or eggs is not illegal, but it is against written eBay policy, making it unlikely that children will be born because of an eBay purchase anytime soon.

ARE YOU DAMNED ANYWAY?

With the advent of eBay, the need to meet face-to-face with the devil in order to sell your soul has become a thing of the past. Over the years, several individuals have made high-profile attempts to sell their—or someone else's—

soul on eBay. As early as 1999, news articles began making reference to souls for sale on eBay, but it was not until one attracted a $400 bid in 2001 that the media started paying significant attention to the implications of such arrangements.

In the 2001 case, the seller was a twenty-year-old Washington University student and the auction proceeded without coming to the attention of the people at eBay who regularly pull such sales. In the final hour of the auction, a buyer from Iowa stepped forward with the winning bid. Unfortunately, the seller was never able to collect on the debt owed him, and when his sale was finally brought to the company's attention, he was suspended from doing business on eBay.

Since at least 2000 the company has had a standard response to such offers: "If the soul does not exist, eBay could not allow the auctioning of a soul, because there would be nothing to sell. However, if the soul does exist, then, in accordance with eBay's policy on human parts and remains, we would not allow the auctioning of human souls."

As one seller pointed out in 2003, however, this policy seems to discriminate based on religious beliefs. While the debate about what constitutes a human soul and who, if anyone, should be allowed to sell one may continue in theological courses everywhere, eBay at least does not seem likely to change its position. Among the auctions it has pulled were attempted sales of the soul of George W. Bush and that of a goldfish.

IF MOM AND DAD DON'T GET IT RIGHT
THERE ARE OTHER OPTIONS

Most people go by the name they were given at birth. Sometimes last names change as the result of marriage, and occasionally a nickname will attach itself to a person, but, for the most part, like it or not, people stick with the name they were given. Except for one enterprising woman from Knoxville, Tennessee. Item number 5568750040 went up for sale on March 25, 2005, offering the winner the right to legally change thirty-three-year-old Terri Ilagan's name for life.

The seller assured potential bidders she was in good health and that the purchase was an excellent long-term investment. Whether the name was used to advertise a product, memorialize a loved one, honor a lost love, or celebrate a favorite cartoon character, the seller agreed to take up to three names (first, middle, and last) to be determined by the winning bidder.

According to the sales pitch furnished by the woman formerly known as Terri, "Every time I go to the bank, pay with a credit card, go to the gym, go to the doctor, write a check, enter a contest, buy airline tickets, or just meet new people on a daily basis, the name you picked will be mentioned and exposed!" Terri's exposure began as soon as the ad was posted. The auction was featured in newspapers across the country and the seller found herself being interviewed by radio and television stations from Atlanta to Los Angeles.

The auction was scheduled to run for only three days but was pulled by eBay ten minutes before it was first set to end due to, according to the seller, "a technicality." The second auction also ran for only three days and ended with a winning bid of $15,199 from GoldenPalace.com. According to the seller, who has since been renamed GoldenPalace.com, the purchase of her name qualified as a business expense for the Web site since it was advertising, and was therefore entirely tax-deductible.

LOSING YOUR VIRGINITY

The ad first appeared on eBay's UK site and read: "Eighteen-year-old university student looking to sell virginity. Never lost it due to lesbianism." This offering was submitted by eighteen-year-old Rosie Reed who needed to raise cash to help with the £15,000 (US$27,500) debt she had racked up while in college.

When eBay pulled the ad almost immediately, Rosie was not deterred. She reposted the proposition on her own Web page and was inundated with more than two thousand requests from around the world. The British tabloid *News of the World* paid to be granted exclusive rights to her story and reported that Rosie said, "It started as a joke and ended up as why not?"

The winning bidder was a forty-four-year-old divorced father of two who paid Rosie £8,400 (US$15,400) for the privilege of defrocking her. The man subsequently went into hiding after the *News of the World* published the story. After the deal was consummated, Rosie was quoted as saying, "It was horrible. . . . I felt nervous and scared." The buyer is not likely to emerge anytime soon, as there are reports that Madonna is currently working on a movie based on Rosie's story. No word yet on when we can expect to see the story on the big screen.

MOVING BEYOND A VIRTUAL GIRLFRIEND

One of the phenomena spawned by the rise of the Internet is online dating. In September of 2003 a twenty-two-year-old college junior had a brainstorm after watching the 1980s movie *Can't Buy Me Love*—in which a high school student pays a cheerleader $1,000 a month to date him. She decided to forgo the dog and pony show of a typical romance and, instead, she offered herself as an "Imaginary Girlfriend" to the highest bidder.

In exchange for payment from the highest bidder, this original "Imaginary Girlfriend" promised to pen four letters and send along a picture to her new "boyfriend." She also suggested the "boyfriend" break up with her so she could write a final letter begging him to take her back. This first auction attracted 16,000 hits and a final sale price of $41. So successful was her first auction that she tried it again, this time attracting 20,000 hits and a final sale price of $81.

These sales in turn gave rise to a host of copycat imaginary girlfriends, and at one time eBay had more than sixty-five "girlfriends" offering a range of imaginary "services." Eventually the trend got a little too hot to handle, so in February of 2004 eBay stepped in and began removing the auctions after determining that the listings had moved into territory that was "clearly inappropriate."

If you missed out on the auctions but are still looking for imaginary love, take heart. There are several sites independent of eBay where one can purchase an imaginary girlfriend. For the dedicated eBayer, I LOVE MY IMAGINARY GIRLFRIEND bumper stickers still appear for sale from time to time.

HOW ABOUT THIS BOOB?

Tawny Peaks was an exotic dancer working at the Diamond Dolls Night Club in Clearwater, Florida, when she became famous as the result of a lawsuit filed against her and her employer. According to the plaintiff, a patron of the club, he was attending a bachelor party when Tawny's breast hit him. The aggrieved party claimed he suffered whiplash as a result of Tawny's 69HH breast smacking him in the face.

The patron stated her accoutrements were like "two cement blocks," and he filed suit in Pinellas County Court asking for $15,000 in damages. Eventually, both sides agreed to arbitration and the case, which came to be known as "Assault with a Breast," ended up on *The People's Court* in front of former New York City mayor Ed Koch. Koch ruled in Tawny's favor, finding the breasts "too soft to inflict pain."

Peaks, who appeared on the cover of a 1999 *Playboy*, had her implants removed in 2002 after retiring from show business. EBay auction 5561537389 offered one of those implants autographed by the former exotic dancer.

Bidding began at $1, and, as the breast attracted more and more attention from the media and viewing public, the price skyrocketed. In total, 575,125 people visited the auction during its run on eBay. After 66 bids the notorious eBay connoisseur GoldenPalace.com walked away victorious, agreeing to pay $16,766 for the treasure. The casino also received an autographed copy of the court complaint. There is no word yet on how the implant will be put to use.

TILL DEATH DO YOU PART

Tired of the dating scene and ready to settle down? A twenty-four-year-old woman from Birmingham, England, had a solution: buy her hand in marriage. According to the advertisement placed on eBay UK, entitled "Buy an entrepreneur wife," the seller claimed to be an Internet entrepreneur who had met all of her career goals but had not yet found that perfect someone.

Auction number 1677522500 went live Dec 13, 2001, and had a reserve price of £250,000 (more than US $450,000). The seller stipulated that her new husband be male, a British citizen, between the ages of twenty-four and thirty-five, and meet basic health requirements. The winning bidder would also be required to sign a prenuptial agreement. Bidding was intense, but eBay pulled the auction about twenty-four hours after the listing went live because the company viewed the sale as "unethical." By then the auction had been bid up to £10,000,000.

Although her listing was removed from eBay, that did not stop the seller. She turned to eBay UK rival QXL to help her find a mate. There the auction continued and, despite hoax bidding which at one point pushed the sale up into the billions of pounds, the seller believed, when the auction ended, that she had found a legitimate bidder willing to pay £251,000 for her hand.

Alas, the story did not end happily ever after. Unfortunately, the winning bid turned out to be a hoax after all. Although the man she thought had placed the bid did in fact exist, when confronted, he knew nothing of the auction. Apparently he'd just returned penniless from traveling overseas.

Profit from Someone Else

Lawyers, consultants, doctors, and dentists—all of them make their living off of things that happen to other people. Likewise, on eBay, one of the truest recipes for achieving fame and fortune is to auction off something that belongs to someone else.

Often these auctions come about as a result of a divorce or a spat between a couple. One sure way to get revenge on a misbehaving partner is to sell his or her stuff on eBay. Did an ex-wife leave behind a wedding dress or a collection of Beanie Babies? Maybe your philandering husband made the mistake of registering his car under your name? If you are willing to air your dirty laundry in public, then you could be well on your way to hosting your own legendary auction.

Sometimes selling someone else means, literally, selling someone else. Maybe you are thinking about placing Grandma in a nursing home but want to explore all the options? Perhaps you know a famous person whose time you can sell off to the highest bidder? As the following case studies underscore, creativity counts!

You'll need to make sure to provide as many of the lurid details as you can when selling something that belongs to someone else, and, most important of all, make sure to keep your sense of humor. As many celebrities can attest, the media can be a fickle beast.

HEADED FOR A NASTY DIVORCE

According to the seller of eBay UK item 4150791231, his wife had up and left him to go on vacation with another man. The jilted husband's solution? "I intend to flog all of her more personal stuff here on eBay. Starting with the sl*g's underwear." So began one of the most famous of eBay revenge stories.

Within twelve hours of the unveiling of the auction of the used dainties on May 11, 2004, more than 25,000 people had tuned in. There shoppers were greeted with a pic-

ture of the auctioneer's wife along with a description of how, on the seller's dime, she had run off to travel the world with someone else. In addition, the seller provided his audience with a link to a Web site where he detailed more of his partner's indiscretions.

Fifty-one bids pushed the asking price up to £245 (US$480) before eBay pulled the item for violating the company's policy against hawking used undergarments. Undeterred, the seller relisted some underwear he claimed were new and, therefore, not prohibited. Obviously still bitter, the seller added, "Anyway, as these knickers are some of the rare ones that she's NOT had round her ankles, I would like them to go to a new home." This offering also violated various eBay policies, including the posting of links to outside sources and the offering of items not belonging to the seller. There is no word on where these panties finally landed.

WORSE THAN COAL FOR CHRISTMAS

As the holiday season comes around each year, so do the threats from parents to their kids: "If you aren't good, Santa is going to leave you only coal this Christmas!" In 2004, two parents in Texas acted on that age-old threat and in so doing struck fear into the hearts of children everywhere. This sale will almost certainly add to the repertoire parents have on hand to keep their children in line.

Fed up with their children's antics, a certain mom and dad went to the closet, pulled out a new Nintendo DS system they had planned to give the kids for Christmas, and put it up for sale on eBay. The title of eBay auction 8157047854 read, "Bad Children get no Nintendo DS. Santa will skip our house this year." The sellers further added: "Three undeserving boys have crossed the line."

Worldwide press attention ensued, debate raged about whether this was an appropriate way to punish children, and millions of people tuned into eBay to view the auction. Because of the massive amount of attention the sale received, numerous false bids were placed, reaching into the hundreds of thousands of dollars; it was only after the third listing of the item that a sale actually went through.

The final sale price for the Nintendo DS and three games: $5,300. The actual retail price for the items was about $300. The winning bidder was GoldenPalace.com, and, in this case, the casino stipulated that its winning bid be donated to a charity. The seller agreed to use the proceeds to purchase a new heater for the family's church and to pay for other renovations. A GoldenPalace.com spokesperson said the Nintendo was donated to a needy family in Houston.

DEAL OF A LIFETIME

Normally the purpose of an eBay auction is to capture as much money as possible for an item. Not so for the seller of a Lotus Esprit Turbo listed as item number 4556985749 on eBay UK. The car, valued at £25,000 (almost US$50,000), was put up for sale with a "buy it now" price of 50 p (a little less than US$1) by the wife of UK shock jock Tim Shaw.

Known as "Prankster Tim" in Birmingham, England, the radio personality was doing his on-air show one day when he propositioned model Jodie Marsh, telling her that he was going to leave his wife and two kids for her. The DJ had previously angered his wife by saying on-air that when the two of them had sex he thought of her sister. The Jodie Marsh comment was apparently the proverbial straw that broke the camel's back.

In her two-line advertisement on eBay Shaw's outraged wife stated that she needed to get rid of the car immediately, "ideally in the next 2–3 hours before my cheating arsehole husband gets home to find it gone." She instructed potential buyers to bid only if they could pick up the vehicle in Birmingham that evening, and she assured them that because she was listed in the logbook, that technically she could sell the automobile. The car sold within five minutes and the buyer arrived in time to drive off before hubby returned from his radio gig that evening. According to the wife, the marriage was beyond repair.

ONE WAY TO UPSTAGE THE BRIDE ON HER WEDDING DAY

Almost everyone has, at one point or another, been invited to an event he or she just would rather not attend. Most people try to come up with as creative and kind an excuse as possible. But when a man from Aberdeen, Scotland, was invited to a wedding he did not wish to grace with his presence, he took a less subtle approach. He put the invitation up for sale on eBay.

Citing as the reason for the sale his dislike for the fiancée of the friend who had invited him (his exact words were "she's a dog"), the seller told potential bidders, "No one will know you're not me except the groom, and he'll be so pissed trying to forget his new wife's a dog he won't notice."

When the auction hit the newswires, every bride-to-be in the United Kingdom was praying that it was not an invitation to her wedding that had been put up for sale. Bidding for item 5527273221 on eBay UK shot to more than a million pounds until controls were put in to verify eligible bidders. One and a quarter million people flooded the listing in the nine days it was a live item.

Then, with a day and a half of bidding remaining and journalists from around the world following the event, the seller pulled the invitations. In his explanation he said he was not actually a friend of the groom but, rather, an ex of the bride, whom he claimed he still loved. According to the note the seller attached to the item before he canceled bidding, the auction had gotten her attention and she had called him the previous evening. He decided he was going to attend the wedding after all and try one last time to win her back. Whether this ploy worked remains an open question. The seller, known to the world only as "twinklydog," has not been heard from since.

HOW TO MAKE YOUR WEDDING INVITATIONS A COLLECTIBLE

It appears there are more ways than one for a wedding invitation to become memorable on eBay. Most people are familiar with the story of Jennifer Wilbanks, who became known across the United States as the "Runaway Bride," a nickname inspired by the movie of the same name, starring Julia Roberts and Richard Gere. The week before she was to be married, Wilbanks disappeared from her Duluth, Georgia, home after telling her fiancé she was going out for a jog.

When Wilbanks failed to return, her fiancé notified police and a national search began. Four and a half days later she turned up in New Mexico after calling home. Initially she claimed she had been kidnapped and driven more than a thousand miles from her home, but she quickly recanted. It turns out she "needed some time alone before the wedding."

Wilbanks will likely forever be known as the Runaway Bride, and, with more than eight hundred guests asked to attend the wedding, it was only a matter of time before one of her wedding invitations ended up on eBay. Item 5578195975 was entitled "Jennifer Wilbanks & John Mason Wedding Invitation" and apparently also included a reception card.

According to the advertisement, the item was offered by the child of a couple who had been invited to the ceremony. When some eBay visitors criticized the sale as tacky, the seller responded, "and by the way I was not personally invited to the wedding, my parents were. So stop saying things like I should be ashamed. Hello, if you were me you would be happy to get the money."

Thirty-three thousand people tuned into the auction while it was live, and 24 bids were placed on the item. It sold to GoldenPalace.com for $355. The casino added this invitation to a collection of items it had recently won in a second famous auction, item number 5577585474, "Jennifer Wilbanks Runaway Bride Wedding Kit!" For that sale, which was visited by more than 100,000 people, the seller created a collection of spoof items and a witty description, all of which were designed to "help any nervous bride who wants to get away from all the pressure of getting married."

WHAT'S IN A NAME, ESPECIALLY IF IT IS NOT YOURS?

According to the description of auction number 5557446658, the item would be delivered May 5, 2005. It arrived early. On April 27, a baby girl was born at Charlotte Hungerford Hospital in northwest Connecticut and, through another commercial venture wrought via eBay, she now shares a name with an online casino.

According to the ad placed on eBay and entitled "Name my baby girl due 05/05," the child's parents were having a difficult time coming up with a name and decided, "Why not come to eBay and have the lucky winner of my auction name the baby?"

So up for sale went the right to name the soon-to-be-born baby girl. The ad stipulated that the buyer could choose to give the newborn either a first or a middle name and that the name could not be anything vulgar, extremely geeky, or totally off the wall. In return, the winning bidder could expect a copy of the birth certificate to show that the sellers had upheld their end of the bargain, as well as a picture of the infant.

The auction attracted national news attention and 38 bids. Naming rights were sold to GoldenPalace.com for $15,100. According to the casino's Web page, "Golden Palace.com's mother Melissa says that the money will help pay for the baby's necessities and anything left over will be placed into a trust fund."

Apparently GoldenPalace.com can be either a boy's or a girl's name, as the casino also won auction 5563865831, which gave it the right to name a baby boy due May 17, 2005. In that case the casino exercised the "buy it now" option for $15,000 rather than risk a bidding war. GoldenPalaceDotCom Silverman arrived in good health but two days late on May 19, 2005.

THE BEANIE BABY INCIDENT

It was the passion with which the seller, Steve Kaye, marketed a set of seemingly ordinary Beanie Babies that made auction number 3146042998 famous. Listed in September 2003, the auction was entitled "Collection of 26 Beanie Babies from Ex-Wife," and it drew nearly 1.3 million interested people.

The sales pitch read:

> Let me begin by explaining some very important details, this way I do not get 100's of silly emails asking me to photograph the hind end of some stuffed animals. I DO NOT KNOW crap about these things. These belonged to my ex-wife who had about a 1000 of these Beanie Babies and when she moved, this one box of these got left behind, and now I am selling the goofy little things. Whatever money I make from them will be spent at the local Home Depot on tools and other cool stuff. . . . I am starting the auction at $10 and at that price I figure you all can take a chance. I understand from a friend's wife that people are afraid to get fakes. FAKES? Fake plush toys? I was amazed. I thought people forged money, not children's toys. Well I can only say, that 99% of these goofy toys were bought with my money, from either the local Hallmark Store, or one of the dozen or so Southern Craft/collectibles stores I had to go to on a weekly basis buying these ridiculous toys years ago.

To ensure that his buyers were aware of his knowledge of the topic, the seller added one final warning:

> Final Notice and Disclaimer: I know nothing about these stuffed Beanie Babies. I offer no proof of anything. It is a stuffed animal, get over it! I don't think my ex-wife was in the Black Market Beanie Trade . . . but then again, I didn't know she was having an affair either! Thus no guarantees!

With that, the auction went live. Nonetheless, much to the seller's dismay, the comments did come in, including one telling him that many of the Beanie Babies were probably fake and accused him of being a criminal. In response, the seller shot back:

> WELL [NAME]! I don't CARE! I told everyone in the beginning everything I know and don't know about these STUPID animals! I have an idea for all the people that are so worried about this. . . . Don't BID! I don't care! . . . I have blocked her from my bidder list. . . .

As it turned out, the potential buyer who had made the comment did care. She changed her eBay moniker, bid, and actually won the auction. When the stuffed animals were delivered it turned out that some of the Beanie Babies were, according to the buyer, fakes. At which point the buyer informed an Internet fair trade company, which threatened the seller with legal action and a visit from the

FBI. The seller, who to this day maintains perfect positive feedback with more than 770 positive experiences logged, fired back the following:

> I have no idea who you are, or what your "[complaint]" is. I find your comments threatening and offensive. I don't care what [NAME] is demanding. I am demanding that you no longer email me. As I told him/her, feel free to call the police, FBI, Postal Inspector, and the Freaking Wildlife Organization that governs Blue Stuffed Elephants. . . .

According to the seller, he never refunded the woman's money and, because of all the publicity, he began receiving thousands of emails, many of which were offers to buy him a beer. In response he put up a set of auctions that entitled buyers, for $1.77 ($1.50 plus the cost of postage), to a certificate proclaiming that they did indeed buy him a cold one. He sold more than 1,100 of these certificates before eBay finally put a stop to it.

BETTER THAN GETTING PUT IN A HOME?

Maybe the seller of item 69987688 was worried about the prohibitive cost of nursing homes. Whatever the reason, in February of 1999 one of the first eBay auctions to generate significant media attention went live. In the description of the item entitled "Grandma for sale—Must See!" the seller claimed it was "the auction of the century."

Up for sale was an "authentic grandma" who had lived through two world wars, who loved picking up after people, and who came with dentures and a "coffin for when she dies." Bidding for the grandma, said to be located in California, rocketed from $10 to over a million in just short of two days. EBay pulled the auction shortly thereafter because it is a matter of company policy not to allow the sale of human beings.

Despite eBay's demonstrated unwillingness to allow a seller to auction off a family member, others have not been deterred from trying. On January 9, 2003, a television writer attempted to auction off his family, consisting of his wife and two children, in eBay sale number 2905270846. For $5 million the seller said his family members would change their last name to that of the buyer, and, in addition, everything the seller wrote from that point forward would be credited to the buyer. "You can be an author without the drudgery of actually writing. Imagine the thrill of watching your name flow by hurriedly on television and film credits. . . ." the auction spiel promised.

Similarly, in 2004, a German woman found herself under investigation by the police when she posted an ad putting up for sale her eight-year-old daughter with the sales pitch "You can play with her." The couple who placed a 25.50 euro bid (US$23) on the child also found themselves under police scrutiny. In the end the incident proved to be a bad joke, with an unfortunate use of language, and not a case of child prostitution as some had feared.

GOLF WITH TIGER WOODS, LUNCH WITH WARREN BUFFETT

Finding a celebrity and then auctioning off the privilege of spending time with him or her has long been a staple of charity fund-raisers. With the rise of eBay the opportunity to auction off celebrities has reached a whole new level. Two of the most noteworthy of these types of sales were the opportunity for a foursome to play golf with Tiger Woods and the chance to have lunch with Warren Buffett.

The auction for a golf date with Tiger Woods ran between April 4 and April 12, 2002, and promised the winner of the auction and three of his or her closest friends a chance to play golf with Tiger. Tee time was to be negotiated but would take place on Tiger's home golf course, the Isleworth Country Club in Windermere, Florida. Proceeds were to benefit the Tiger Woods Foundation.

Prospective buyers were required to sign up in advance and put down a $50,000 deposit. Bidding began at $100,000 and by the time it ended thirteen bids had been recorded and someone had agreed to pay $425,000 for the privilege of an afternoon on the links with Tiger Woods. This item remains one of the most expensive ever sold for charity on eBay. Tiger has since auctioned off several other similar experiences, although none has quite approached the price of the 2002 sale.

For those who would rather partake in a power lunch than a round of golf, perhaps the opportunity to sit down with Warren Buffett and seven of your friends at the New

York City steak house Smith & Wollensky is more your style. In May 2004 Warren Buffett auctioned off what was described as "the chance of a lifetime to pick the brain of the one and only Warren Buffett." The proceeds were to benefit the Glide Foundation, a San Francisco service provider for the poor and homeless.

The winning bid of $202,100 came from an anonymous Singapore businessman who upped his donation to an even $250,000, because "the winner liked the cause." Either way, the economy must have been down a bit in 2004, since a similar package sold in 2003 raised $250,100.

EVERY TEENAGE BOY'S FANTASY

If Tiger and Warren are too boring for you then perhaps auction 6528557289, entitled "Win a 'Dream Date' with Carmen Electra," may better appeal to your wild side. Carmen may be married to rock star Dave Navarro, but when Gillette put up the auction to promote its new body spray TAG, the small matter of her technically being off the dating market did not seem to matter. Only those aged fifteen to twenty were eligible to bid, ensuring that Electra, who was thirty-three at the time, would be more than thirteen years older than her male companion on the big night.

The auction began April 27, 2005, with the requirement that any potential buyer under the age of eighteen arrange for someone older to bid for him. (EBay rules prohibit people under the age of eighteen from participating in auctions.) Gillette also required that the winner submit to a background check, be a U.S. resident, and, if under the age of eighteen, be accompanied on the date by a legal guardian. The three-hour rendezvous was to take place in Los Angeles, and the winner would receive, in addition to the date, airfare for two and hotel accommodations.

Bidding began at $500 and quickly skyrocketed. By the time the auction ended, 122 bids had been received and the date with Electra sold for $407,500. All money raised from the auction was to benefit the National Prostate Cancer Coalition.

It should be noted that subsequent research could not confirm that the date ever actually occurred. The winner of the auction had earned multiple negative feedbacks for nonpayment; in one case he responded by blaming his cat, and in another his excuse was that his house had burned down. As for the runner-up, a look at the history of his purchases on eBay shows the recent acquisition of a three-month supply of Rogaine, leading one to surmise that perhaps the bidder did not fall into the age range eligible for participation in the auction.

THE PRICE OF COMPETITION

College athletics are a pricey proposition. Some sports, such as football and basketball, can bring in a significant amount of money to a university's coffers, but most sports yield net financial losses for schools. Just before Thanksgiving in

2002, officials at Dartmouth College made a decision to cut the Ivy League school's swim team in order to save the $212,000 annual cost of the program. Things looked bad for the Dartmouth swimmers until the boyfriend of one of the team members came up with an idea many credit with saving the program: list the team for sale on eBay.

Item number 1976909200 went live December 1, 2002, and asked for an opening bid of $211,000. Half cynical, half nostalgic, the item description featured biographies of many of the team's swimmers, team pictures, and an account of the school's history. The sales pitch claimed, "This is a once-in-a-lifetime opportunity to own a piece of NCAA Division I collegiate memorabilia." Slowly the item began attracting attention and then bids. First Swiminfo.com ran an article, followed by features in the *New York Times*, *Boston Globe*, *Seattle Times*, and *Washington Post*, among others. ESPN's Sports Center featured the story, as did multiple networks on their national evening news.

EBay pulled the team on December 4 after it became apparent that the sellers did not own their offering and Dartmouth officials would not give their blessing to the sale. According to the college's dean, James Larimore, "We simply do not operate that way." That may be true, but the auction sparked a groundswell of support for the program. Hundreds of alumni and others outside the Dartmouth community rallied behind the team, and in January of 2003 the school accepted a proposal that will keep the team in the pool until at least 2013.

WEDDING DRESS GUY

Item 4146756343, which went live on April 23, 2004, is perhaps the most famous of all eBay auctions. Yet based on the item's description, "SIZE 12 WEDDING DRESS/ GOWN NO RESERVE," you would never have guessed there was anything unusual about it. One peek, how-

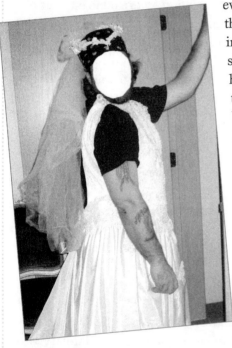

ever, changed everything. Pictured modeling the beaded white size 12 gown, which had formerly belonged to his ex-wife, was bearded and tattooed Larry Star. The three shots of him modeling the dress, coupled with his incredibly humorous account of the outfit's history and why his ex-wife had left him with it, made him an international sensation overnight.

Originally the seller said he hoped to sell the dress and "get enough money for maybe a couple of Mariners tickets and some beer." Instead he received worldwide attention, multiple invitations to appear on the *Today* show, a place in "Yahoo's Netrospective: 10 years, 100 moments of the Web," and more than 18 million visitors to his auction. Because of the sale's notoriety, bidding was limited to preapproved buyers only, and the sale closed with a winning bid of $3,850.

The wedding dress auction has become larger than life and Larry Star has used its fame to remain in the limelight. He has even published a book titled *Bitter, Party of One . . . Your Table Is Ready: Relationship Advice from a Guy Who Has No Business Giving It*, written with the same self-deprecating humor that millions of fans who flocked to his auction have come to expect from the Wedding Dress Guy. He also runs the Web site www.weddingdressguy.com, where you can visit the original auction, read about Larry's ongoing projects—which include appearing at comedy clubs and singing and playing guitar in his band The Buzzcuts—and even purchase t-shirts, ball caps, coffee mugs, and bumper stickers with the now famous photos of Larry in the dress.

AN AMICABLE SEPARATION

Twenty-six million people watched Aaron Beurge choose Helene Eksterowicz as his bride-to-be on the finale of ABC's second season of *The Bachelor*. Twenty-five single women were introduced to Beurge during the series premier, and over an eight-show run the group was gradually winnowed down to two. In the grand finale, in front of millions of viewers, Aaron got down on his knees and slipped a 2.75-carat Harry Winston diamond and platinum ring onto Helene Eksterowicz's finger. She accepted his marriage proposal and the two went off to live in that happy place where reality-show couples go when the cameras are turned off.

In the end, reality caught up with the pair and they turned out not to be as compatible as they had hoped. As for the ring, well what better way to dispose of it than on eBay? The ring, valued at approximately $29,000, went up for sale on February 9, 2004, with a minimum opening bid of $17,500. Even though the story was featured by all of the entertainment and celebrity news outlets, bidding, which was limited to preapproved buyers, got off to a slow start. There were, in fact, no bids on the final morning of the sale.

Ultimately, suitors for the ring were just fashionably late putting in their offers. By the time the auction closed on Thursday evening, 52 bids had been placed, resulting in a final sale price of $28,300. The sale enabled the former couple to avoid a court date during which the fate of the ring would have been decided in arbitration.

As for the auction's winners, they also got a few extra perks. Besides the ring, the high bidder and his fiancée were given the opportunity to meet the former couple in New York City, received shot glasses and t-shirts from

Beurge's restaurant, and were given an autographed copy of the book Eksterowicz wrote with former rival for the bachelor's affections Gwen Gioia, entitled *Nobody's Perfect: What to Do When You've Fallen for a Jerk but You Want to Make It Work.*

Profiting from These Strange Times

Auctions on eBay often mirror real-world news events. Some of the most famous of eBay sales can be directly tied to current events. By being creative and having a nose for finding a special item associated with a news-making phenomenon, you could be on your way to hosting a notorious eBay sale.

Were you in Florida when Elian Gonzalez's raft was disposed of by customs enforcement agents? Can you come up with a funny way to use a stick and a white piece of fabric to poke fun at the French and their wartime inclinations? Do you live in an area prone to natural disasters? If you answered yes to any of these questions or simply have a nose for the news, you may want to pay particular attention to the next few pages.

Many of the creative sales dreamt up by news-savvy eBayers and featured in this lesson have reaped small windfalls for their sellers. Just as the headlines change every day, so too do the items listed for sale on eBay. By linking your auction with the news of the day, the potential for a determined eBayer to profit and make headlines of your own is boundless.

VIVE LA FRANCE!!

Item number 2160749477, titled "Vintage Very Rare WWII French Battle Flag," looked suspiciously like a piece of white cloth fastened to a bamboo stick. It was posted in late winter of 2003 as the United States stood on the brink of war with Saddam Hussein's Iraq and the French government had taken a leadership role among the coalition of nations urging restraint and patience.

Anti-French sentiment was at an all-time high in Washington, D.C., and Congress took the unusual step of registering their displeasure with France by renaming French fries "freedom fries" in the cafeterias that served the Capitol. Perhaps taking a cue from their elected leaders in Washington, a host of eBayers were quick to try to

capitalize on the anti-French sentiment. None attracted more attention than the auction for the "Vintage French battle flag." The seller alleged that his grandmother had obtained the flag during World War II, days after the Normandy Invasion, from a group of elite French commandos who had been hiding in an isolated village since 1939.

With bidding at $16,000 and more than two days remaining until the sale would close, eBay pulled the item, possibly because, according to one poster on the Forum of the *Dallas Digest*, the item was listed internationally and likely "fell foul of the Race Relation Act" by inciting hatred of other nationalities.

Among other anti-French items to turn up on eBay around this time were a French rifle—"It's never been fired and it's been dropped only once"—and numerous "Boycott France" t-shirts and bumper stickers.

In a related incident, one eBayer refused to ship a printer to a winning bidder because the buyer was Canadian. According to Wired.com, David Ingram, a tax consultant from Vancouver, won an auction for a printer but instead of receiving the printer got a message from the seller stating that he or she did not accept bids from Canada, Mexico, France, Germany, or any other country opposed to the United States' efforts in Iraq. According to the same article, although eBay frowns upon posting "overtly political messages," sellers can decide with whom they choose to do business.

PRIME-TIME EXPOSURE

In August 2005, in an effort to reduce tensions with the Palestinians, the Israeli government began forced evacuations of Jewish settlers living in the Gaza Strip and West Bank. As the evacuations progressed, many settlers of the disputed territories left voluntarily, but many others stayed behind. Those who remained forced Israeli troops to physically remove them from their homes and synagogues, and images of these confrontations were broadcast around the world. Knowing that Israeli soldiers would soon be coming to Sanur, their West Bank settlement, one couple was inspired by the prospects of world media attention to put eBay item number 5608812782 up for sale.

For an opening bid of $40,000 the Sanur couple promised one lucky bidder the opportunity to place a banner advertising his or her company, or anything else, on the side of a fortress. The sellers stated that they, along with hundreds of others, would be barricading themselves inside the fortress in an effort to prevent their forced removal from the settlement. Their standoff with the troops would, they guaranteed potential bidders, attract world news coverage. Thus the potential buyer, and the rest of the world, would see the banner advertisement proudly displayed in what, if the purchaser was lucky, might even escalate to a serious armed conflict.

Posted with the auction description was a picture of the fortress with a caption telling potential buyers their advertisement "would go here," along with a picture of the couple, their faces covered, to show that they were indeed in the West Bank. Although the sale made news around the world and, ultimately, pictures of the forced evacuation were broadcast by international media, there were no advertisements hanging from the fortress when soldiers arrived in Sanur. No bids had been received on the item before it made the news, and when the publicity brought the matter to the company's attention eBay quickly pulled the sale.

THE UNDERBELLY OF THE EBAY COMMUNITY

Amadou Bailo Diallo was a twenty-four-year-old Guinea immigrant living in New York City in 1999 when he was killed in a hail of gunfire in front of his apartment by four New York City police officers. Although the four white officers claimed that the African native appeared to be reaching for a gun, Diallo was found to be unarmed. The killing touched off a wave of racially charged anti-police protests in New York City and around the country.

Two years later part of Diallo's apartment door turned up on eBay. The seller claimed to have acquired the relic after hearing it had been removed from the building. According to CNN, which conducted a phone interview with the seller, "the piece of door is about four feet high by six inches wide, and has graffiti messages on it such as 'never again,' 'RIP' and some vulgarities."

The seller, a white man from the South Bronx, began the bidding at $41,000, a figure he arrived at by calculating $1,000 for every bullet fired by the police. The seller claimed half of the proceeds would go to Diallo's family; yet family members were not contacted prior to the auction going live and said even if they had been they never would have accepted the money. Outraged New Yorkers, activists, and, most significantly, Diallo's family contacted eBay demanding that the sale be stopped, and eBay quickly complied.

EBay has a strict policy allowing it to "remove items and refund listing fees when the item or description graphically portrays violence or victims of violence, and lacks substantial social, artistic or political value." In addition to the Diallo case, eBay has used this policy to put a stop to among others, the sales of the fingernails of a serial killer, Nazi paraphernalia, and a Web address named after the woman who drowned her children in Texas.

WHAT PRICE THE VOTE?

In the 2000 presidential election the entire U.S. population saw how an individual vote might make all the difference in the world. Yet, even before it was clear that the 2000 election would be a squeaker, one eBayer made national news for trying to sell his vote in that year's presidential election.

Item number 410721373, entitled "Vote of one U.S. Citizen," went live on August 15, 2000. It was put up by a seller who said he or she lived in Maryland and stated, "Why should the American citizen be left out? Congressmen and Senators regularly sell THEIR votes to the highest bidder. Democracy for sale!"

According to the auction description, not only would the winning bidder get the opportunity to choose his or her favorite presidential candidate; he or she would also be able to dictate the entire slate of selections to be made all the way down to local ordinance laws. The item was bid up to $10,000 before eBay put a halt to the auction. According to a CNN article about the sale, "Vote selling and purchasing violates Maryland and U.S. laws." Nevertheless, this first sale sparked a trend, and eBayers have been attempting, unsuccessfully, to sell their votes in various elections ever since. This phenomenon is not limited to the United States; news articles written about citizens' attempts to sell their votes on eBay have also appeared in both Britain and Australia.

TREASURE FROM HEAVEN

When the Mir Space Station came crashing to earth in March 2001, much of the 143-ton space vessel disintegrated upon entry into the earth's atmosphere. The rest plunged into the Pacific Ocean somewhere between New Zealand and Chile. The unlikely prospect that pieces of debris could be found, however, did not stop several eBayers from putting up for sale pieces of what they claimed to be recovered wreckage from the craft.

Within hours of the crash, the first of the auctions appeared on the auction site, and over the next day nearly two dozen similar sales appeared. One auction, item 1126603700, was for a bolt a seller from Indiana "found laying next to my van when I left for work this morning. I'm pretty sure it wasn't there when I got home from work last night, so I think the only logical explanation is that some of the Mir debris did come down over Indiana." Another item, according to *Wired Magazine*, was described as looking "suspiciously like a ball of duct tape and wire." In fact, that is exactly what the seller said it was in his description—probably he meant to poke fun at the constant repairs that were made to Mir during the last few years of its orbit.

While the descriptions of the two alleged Mir items were written to make it apparent to all viewers that the sales were jokes, several other auctions were put forward by people trying to make a quick buck off the more trusting members of the eBay community. One piece of debris that was bid up to $4,500 was being sold by an individual who claimed to have been on a chartered fishing vessel in the South Pacific when the "authentic Mir remains" came crashing down near his boat. Somehow, amazingly, despite his remote location, he was able to post the auction within a couple of hours of Mir's descent to earth.

EBay was quick to react to the problem and pulled all of the Mir "relics." According to the company, even if someone actually did possess a true piece of Mir, the Russian government would still be the rightful owner and therefore the seller could not be allowed to post the item.

ONE SOLUTION TO THE RED STATE–BLUE STATE DIVIDE

On November 7, 2000, the citizens of the United States attempted to elect a president. Days after voting ended the world still was not certain whether George W. Bush or Albert Gore Jr. would become the nation's forty-third president, and the American populace was growing restless. As pundits debated the merits of various lawsuits and strategies being pursued by both parties, one enterprising eBayer took matters into his own hands. He put the presidency up for sale.

Item number 497945868 went live at 9:50 a.m. PST on Monday, November 13, and remained posted on eBay for a mere four and a half hours. The author of the auction stated, "Due to the recent ballot confusion in Florida the

Presidential election process has been cancelled for this term. It has now been granted to the common citizen the chance to be President." Bidders jumped on the opportunity, and by the time the auction was pulled the asking price had jumped to $99,999,999.

Although some cynics believe the candidate with the deepest pockets wins elections, the ad was obviously a joke. Nevertheless, the sale received worldwide attention because it served as a metaphor for the uncertainty and frustration that ensued because of the delay in declaring a winner to the 2000 election. As Linda Harrison pointed out in her column for the United Kingdom's *The Register*, at least when the bidding on eBay ended there would be a clear victor.

PROFITING FROM ABERCROMBIE & FITCH'S DEBACLE

In 2002 the retail icon Abercrombie & Fitch landed itself in hot water for peddling t-shirts deemed by many to be offensive and racist. The shirts featured caricatures of Asians wearing pointed hats, with sayings such as WONG BROTHERS LAUNDRY SERVICE—TWO WONGS CAN MAKE IT WHITE. As soon as the line of clothing hit the market it sparked widespread complaints by customers and political action groups. Abercrombie & Fitch apologized and pulled the merchandise from its stores.

The widespread attention generated by the public protests apparently made the shirts "collectible," and immediately after they were pulled from store shelves they began showing up on eBay. A week after they were taken out of circulation, a gray extra-large t-shirt bearing the offending slogan that had originally sold for $15.99 went for $249 on eBay. According to the seller, he purchased the shirt because "as soon as you see the word 'banned,' it means something's valuable. It's humorous, and everything like that gets blown out of proportion."

This was the only sale of this particular shirt to occur on eBay, because the company, seeking to avoid being dragged into the controversy, promptly removed and banned other auctions of the same item. EBay also notified the buyer of the $249 shirt that the company would not facilitate the sale, leaving the fate of the item to be determined outside of normal eBay channels.

NO SUCH THING AS A FREE CONCERT?

In the spring of 2005, singer, producer, occasional actor, and political activist Bob Geldof announced plans to stage Live 8 concerts meant to "highlight the ongoing problem of global poverty and debt." The concerts were to be free to the public and modeled after the 1985 Live Aid concerts that had made Geldof a household name.

The main concert was to take place on July 2 in London, with simultaneous shows also scheduled in Philadelphia, Paris, Rome, South Africa, and Berlin. While the London show was slated to feature a reunited Pink Floyd, Paul McCartney, Madonna, ColdPlay, R.E.M., and U2, among others, in the weeks leading up to the concert neither the star power of these bands nor the issues organizers hoped to draw attention to were the main stories making news. Instead, eBay found itself in the headlines when the tickets that were distributed for free for the London concert were auctioned off for as much as $2,000 apiece.

To Geldof these sales smacked of corporate profiteering and, never one to mince words, he called the auction site, among other things, "electronic pimps." EBay tried to make nice with Geldof, offering to match sales of the tickets with donations to charity, but Geldof flatly refused the offer, accused the auction site of making money "off the world's poorest people," and called for a worldwide boycott of eBay. EBayers siding with Geldof then flooded the site and placed astronomical bids on the tickets with no intention of paying, making it virtually impossible for sellers to successfully complete their sales. Following the public outcry, eBay eventually relented and pulled down all auctions for the charity concerts, ending the public relations nightmare.

IT IS SEAWORTHY, SORT OF

Elian Gonzalez was a little boy from Cuba who, with his mother, stepfather, and nine other people, boarded a raft and attempted to float to freedom in the United States. Along the way the immigrants encountered rough seas and Elian's mother and stepfather drowned. Elian was found two days later in an inner tube three miles off the coast of Florida. He became famous when his father demanded that Elian be returned to Cuba and a custody battle ensued between the child's relatives living in Florida and his father. Eventually the U.S. government and Janet Reno stepped in and removed the boy from his U.S. custodians. The incident outraged many Cuban Americans and might very well have cost Al Gore Florida and thus the entire presidential election in 2000.

The event also generated one of the most famous eBay auctions of all time. Item number 319392299 was titled "100% Genuine raft used by Elian!" with the seller claiming he was selling the actual craft used by the child on his infamous flight from Cuba. "The raft is still in the Govt.

warehouse where I purchased it, but it will be cleared for release on June 1," the seller stated.

Bidding reached $10 million and the seller even offered a 1–800 number for interested parties to call with any questions they might have. Despite these assurances, eBay eventually stopped the auction because the seller could not provide sufficient documentation to eBay to verify how he had purchased the raft or even whether the raft actually existed. This auction spawned numerous takeoffs that also generated a fair amount of publicity, including "Air in a bottle from Elian Gonzalez hometown," "ELIAN! Hair retrieved from trash-bin in FLA," and an "AUTHENTIC Drawing by Elian Gonzales" supposedly created while the toddler was in child custody following his rescue at sea.

THE FLAG THAT FLEW OVER THE PENTAGON ON 9/11

On March 4, 2005, auction number 3962513751 went live on eBay and almost immediately generated intense debate about what items are and are not appropriate to put up for sale. Advertised as a piece of American history, the item was alleged to be the American flag that had flown on a construction crane next to the Pentagon during the terrorist attacks of 9/11. The flag was framed and offered along with a picture of it flying on that fateful day, the text of George W. Bush's address to the nation, and the names of all those who had perished at the Pentagon.

The seller of the item identified himself in the auction

as David Nicholson and said he had found the flag in a set of boxes given to his auction house in May of 2002. With the flag was a note from an employee of the construction company that had owned the crane, stating that this was the flag that had flown on 9/11 and had appeared in numerous pictures documenting the scene in the aftermath of the attacks.

Despite several previous offers, Nicholson said he held on to the flag out of respect for the victims and occasionally loaned it out to museums and schools for display. But Nicholson had developed kidney cancer and said he needed to raise money to help with his treatment and to support his family.

Americans across the country bitterly debated the sale. Many felt it was unconscionable to make a profit off the tragedy while others sympathized with Nicholson's plight. The auction attracted 208 bids and ended with a final sale price of $371,000. In the end, the winning bidder refused to pay when questions about the flag's authenticity were raised by the very construction company upon whose crane it had allegedly flown.

The flag was then relisted and managed a final sale price of only $25,000. The winning bidder in the second auction was the chairman of the Loudon (VA) County School Board. He planned to fly it at a new elementary school named for two of the victims who had been aboard the plane that crashed into the Pentagon.

Because of his disappointment over the sale price in the second auction, the seller filed a lawsuit against the construction company for the difference between the first and second auction prices, alleging that their "intentional interference" had caused him to lose out on $346,000. Covering all of his bases, Nicholson also sued the employee who had donated the boxes and written the letter about the flag.

THE LIGHTER SIDE OF BANKRUPTCY

After the gravity of the Enron fiasco became known, one place where the value of Enron-related material did not plummet was on eBay. While shares of Enron were selling on the New York Stock Exchange for pennies, those holding commemorative certificates for a single share of Enron stock were peddling them for $90 apiece on eBay. "Perhaps, only coincidentally," said an article in *City Beat*, "the $90 price virtually matches the all-time high share price of Enron's publicly traded stock." When someone coupled a stock certificate with the company's handbook on ethics, bidding on eBay shot to $300.

Enron-emblazoned baseballs, company paperweights, and even an Enron hand-cranked paper shredder were just a few of the thousands of Enron-related products being sold by former employees in the days following the energy giant's collapse. Among some of the auctions that generated the most attention:

- An Enron coffee cup that on the front said ENRON RETIREMENT PLANNING and, on the back, WHO DECIDES WHERE TO INVEST YOUR MONEY? YOU. The winning bid: $152.50.
- A set of ten Enron Stress Balls: $44 and up.

our | **values**

respect

We treat others as we would like to be treated ourselves. We do not tolerate abusive or disrespectful treatment. Ruthlessness, callousness, and arrogance don't belong here.

integrity

We work with customers and prospects openly, honestly, and sincerely. When we say we will do something, we will do it; when we say we cannot or will not do something, then we won't do it.

communication

We have an obligation to communicate. Here, we take the time to talk to one another…and to listen. We believe that information is meant to move and that information moves people.

excellence

We are satisfied with nothing less than the very best in everything we do. We will continue to raise the bar for everyone. The great fun here will be for all of us to discover just how good we can really be.

- Bicycle jerseys emblazoned with Enron's official corporate values—respect, integrity, excellence, and communication—went for $100 and up.
- Enron risk management handbooks, which include tips on increasing creditworthiness and timing reported earnings, sold for $225 and up.
- A sterling-silver key chain with the company's logo made by Tiffany went for nearly $300.
- Enron training manuals for new employees: $200 and up.
- Finally, Enron job termination papers: $9.99 each.

HOW TO GET NOTICED AT THE YACHT CLUB

Since the fall of the Soviet Union there has been great concern about Soviet weapons and technology falling into the wrong hands. It was only a matter of time before some of these items ended up on eBay. A seller claiming to be a Russian citizen with a Ph.D. in international law offered for sale in auction 142918447 a genuine Russian military patrol boat. He assured potential bidders he was also an expert in the operation of the item and would provide the winning bidder with the proper training needed to navigate the vessel.

The seller did not go into much detail about the boat or how he had acquired it, saying simply, "It is a superb vessel," and, "I understand with a purchase this large questions would arise." The craft was said to be located in

Baltimore, Maryland, and the seller urged potential bidders to contact him with their inquiries. The item attracted 44 bids reaching $85,100, but this did not meet the minimum required by the seller for a successful sale.

Perhaps owing to the attention it received in the media, the boat never resurfaced on eBay. Despite not selling, the auction was recognized with a number of awards by news columnists. A writer at the UK online tabloid *The Daily Mirror* ranked the item the eleventh most bizarre eBay auction of all time, and Kevin Gibson of Askmen.com rated it the second "coolest item" ever sold on eBay, right behind Brett Favre's house. The boat's location and the whereabouts of the Russian seller are today unknown.

Anything Linked to Celebrity

Do you have something a celebrity once touched? There could be a big payday and significant media exposure in your future if you do. No formula for creating a legendary eBay auction is more time-tested than a sale revolving around a celebrity.

The more bizarre the item you have, the more likely it is to get you in the news. Granted, in the following pages a couple of the items associated with celebrity are not particularly bizarre, but they are of historic value, such as the contract for selling Babe Ruth to the Yankees or Captain Kirk's commander's chair. Since you may not have the luck to stumble upon treasures of such obvious worth, you are probably better off creating an auction that is tied to a celebrity in a more offbeat way.

Things that celebrities use, leave their DNA on, and then dispose of, for example, tend to have high retail value and attract significant media interest. As you will learn in the case studies that follow, sometimes used gum, dirty bathwater, or a half-eaten piece of French toast can sell for a small fortune and attract extensive news coverage in the process.

You might also want to be on the lookout for items associated with celebrity troubles. A used pregnancy test or a bashed-in front car grille from a wrecked celebrity vehicle, for example, can bring top dollar.

There is no clearer way to highlight the link between eBay and pop culture than by examining what items belonging to which celebrity are selling for the most money. A plunge in the amount of money people are willing to pay for items associated with a particular celebrity will usually coincide with that celebrity's fall from the top of the A-list. As you will learn in the following pages, there is an unending public fascination with celebrity, and selling the trash of the rich and famous can bring you fortune and fame. Who knows, perhaps it will even one day lead to your finding a bottle of water you did not finish being posted for sale by some up-and-coming eBay seller.

TINKERBELLE AND PARIS

When hotel-heiress-turned-reality-television-star Paris Hilton is seen in public it is often with her pet Chihuahua, Tinkerbelle. The pint-sized pup became known to millions of viewers across the country through her critically acclaimed performances on the reality show circuit, starring alongside her owner in the three (to date) *Simple Life* seasons.

When the dog went missing in August of 2004, Paris was reportedly distraught and the search for the dog was national news. In her efforts to find the pooch, Paris even turned to a psychic. She also tried more traditional tactics of finding lost dogs, including offering a reward and posting lost dog signs around Hollywood Hills. It did not take long for one of these signs to appear for sale on eBay.

Item number 4031803051 was a pink piece of poster paper plastered with images of Tinkerbelle and her owner. The sign advertised a $5,000 reward, provided a number to call for individuals who might have located the pup, and implored, PLEASE HELP. THIS DOG IS LIKE A CHILD TO ME.

The story had a happy ending. About a week after Tinkerbelle was reported missing she was found in perfect health. Reports indicate that the dog had been staying with Paris's grandparents and the Hollywood icon simply forgot. As for the poster, it sold for $132.50. In reference to the poster's sale, Hilton reportedly commented, "They took them all down. I saw it on eBay. That was so mean!"

THE PIANO MAN'S APPEARANCE ON EBAY

On April 25, 2004, Billy Joel crashed his 1967 Citroën into the home of a ninety-three-year-old woman in Bayville, New York. Joel was apparently returning to his Long Island estate at around four in the afternoon when he lost control of his car on the rain-slicked road and slammed into the house. The next day the car's battered front grille turned up on eBay.

Item number 3812432670, the front grille of Billy Joel's wrecked automobile, was offered by a reporter from the New York radio station WBLI. The reporter had allegedly retrieved the debris when he went out to the scene of the accident to cover the story. According to the auction description, "This is a collectible for the biggest Billy Joel fan out there." The piece of wreckage included the buckled grille, two emblems, and "actual dirt from 409 Bayville Rd. (the house/victim)."

According to police spokespeople, it is not illegal to remove debris from the scene of an accident once police conclude their investigation. Since Joel did not want the debris returned there was no legal reason that it could not be sold by the radio station. WBLI said all money raised from the sale would go to Long Island charities.

Proving once again that one man's trash is another's treasure, the item attracted 77 bids and bumped up the sale price from a starting offer of $50 to $1,075. Yet at least one organization did not find the auction a laughing matter.

Although there was no evidence that alcohol or drugs were involved in the crash, MADD (Mothers Against Drunk Driving) said, "We see [the auction] as a nasty stunt."

TO SOME, THE HOLY GRAIL

Star Trek fans are notorious for their devotion to the franchise. For many of the most die-hard fans, *Star Trek* is less a show and more a way of life. Trekkies attend conventions where they meet other fans and greet one another in Klingon (*Star Trek* speak), stand in line for hours to meet their favorite *Star Trek* actors, and, of course, collect all things related to *Star Trek*.

On June 27, 2002, what many consider to be the holy grail of the *Star Trek* franchise appeared for sale on eBay: Captain Kirk's command chair. If any one item can represent the phenomenon that is *Star Trek*, it is this chair. Unlike most auctions on eBay, the chair was sold in a live bidding process that took place in Los Angeles and was conducted by the auctioneer "Profiles in History." EBay users were able to follow along from home and, if they had registered in advance, they could participate in the auction action.

Unfortunately, for most fans who coveted the prize chair, the price was out of reach. The auction opened at $80,000 and by the time it had ended 29 bids later, the chair went where no other piece of *Star Trek* memorabilia had gone before: $265,000.

WANT TO CATCH THE SAME FLU PAUL McCARTNEY HAD?

When Ian Mears met Paul McCartney in April of 2003, the rocker was battling a bug that caused the cancellation of the second date of his first British tour in a decade. A couple of days later, Ian came down with what he claimed was the same virus that had plagued Sir Paul. According to an interview conducted by London's *Daily Star*, Ian said, "I had no cold on the Saturday, then on Sunday I spent most of the afternoon with Paul and by Tuesday I too had a cold." Naturally, Ian went to eBay UK and turned what most people would call a curse into brief, worldwide notoriety.

Ian offered potential buyers a couple of ways to catch Paul's cold. His pitch promised: "The highest bidder will receive a resealable bag that I will cough into; or if preferred, they can have a plastic container full of mucus." Most people will go out of their way to avoid getting sick; still the auction did attract a couple of bids and reached £1.20 before the media got ahold of it. Following the attention, eBay moved quickly and pulled the sale, since it was in violation of their policy against selling anything containing human DNA.

Despite his auction being canceled, Ian received worldwide attention. In January of 2004, the attempted sale was rewarded with a ranking of number 14 in *Business 2.0*'s annual "101 Dumbest Moments in Business," which chronicles "the most shameful, dishonest, and just plain stupid moments of the past year."

BEST LIVER?

George Best may not be a household name in the United States, but in many other parts of the world, and particularly in Great Britain, he is the equivalent of Mickey Mantle. A star soccer player for Northern Ireland and Manchester United, Best is widely considered the greatest football star ever to have come out of the British Isles. Best was also known to be a hard-drinking partier whose lifestyle probably ended his career early and forced him to undergo a liver transplant in 2002 at the age of fifty-four. He died on November 25, 2005.

EBay UK item number 2785192105 went up for sale on February 10, 2004, and was titled "George Best's Liver." The seller offered one lucky sports fan the opportunity to own the soccer star's former liver, which the seller claimed he had kept on ice since 2002 when it was "recovered from the incinerator organ bin at London's Cromwell Hospital." The seller was careful to warn would-be buyers that although the liver was in good condition, it was not "suitable for transplant."

The item certainly violated all sorts of eBay policies, including but not limited to the prohibitions against selling items containing human DNA and selling stolen property, but it was the seller—not eBay—who took the item off the market a couple of hours after it was listed. The liver shown in the picture accompanying the auction description looked more like a bloated kidney, and one too large to be human. The abruptness with which the seller ended the auction left many wondering if perhaps the item was not genuine.

BRITNEY SPEARS AND THE PRICE OF CELEBRITY: PART I

When Britney Spears spit out a piece of used chewing gum in the foyer of a London hotel in February of 2004, it probably never crossed her mind that someone would retrieve it. That someone would pay good money for the sticky wad and that this purchase would spark a craze for collecting the discarded gum of celebrities would have seemed almost beyond belief. Yet, thanks to eBay, these incredible things came to pass.

The first piece of Britney's gum showed up on eBay UK in August of 2004 as item number 4031923152. Initially, the seller's main hook line was that he guaranteed DNA

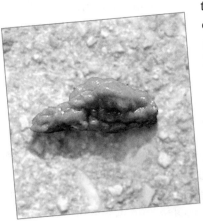

testing would authenticate that the piece of gum truly came from Britney's mouth. But this language violated eBay's policy against the sale of anything containing human DNA, and the seller was forced to briefly pull the item. The gum returned almost immediately without any mention of lingering DNA from the pop diva's saliva.

Following the sale, more of Britney's trash was put up for sale. At one point, two dozen alleged pieces of Britney's gum, the remains of a cigarette supposedly smoked by Britney, and one of her half-finished bottles of water littered eBay's site. The gum belonging to the seller who started the trend sold for £140 (roughly US$250) and inspired Spears's publicist, Leslie Sloane Zelnick, to respond: "This is an all-time low. Anything is possible, I have come to realize, and I do think it's pathetic." While she was right about anything being possible, one wonders what Zelnick would have said about the low reached by the auction of a more intimate item that materialized the following year.

BRITNEY SPEARS AND THE PRICE OF CELEBRITY: PART II

While chewing gum used and discarded by Britney Spears may have been all the rage in 2004, 2005 turned up something of an even more personal nature for sale on eBay: the alleged positive home pregnancy test confirming that the star was carrying a baby. The test bearing the good news was allegedly found in a trash bin in the bathroom of an unnamed hotel in Los Angeles where Spears and her husband, Kevin Federline, had stayed. The pregnancy test was initially sold to Canada's radio station HOT 89.9 by a "connection" the station had at the hotel.

Despite the fact that rumors of her pregnancy had been

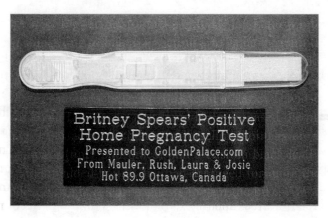

Britney Spears' Positive
Home Pregnancy Test
Presented to GoldenPalace.com
From Mauler, Rush, Laura & Josie
Hot 89.9 Ottawa, Canada

swirling for weeks, the radio station did not leak word of its possession of the urine-soaked stick until after Britney and Kevin had publicly announced that they were indeed expecting a child. At that point the station put the test up for sale on eBay and quickly generated a firestorm of publicity. Unfortunately, the item violated eBay's policy against selling anything containing human DNA, and, unlike the bubble gum incident, there was no reprieve.

The radio station then moved the sale of Britney's home pregnancy test to its own Web site where, over the course of a two-week auction, more than 800 bids were received on the item. According to the station's Web site, staff worked overtime to separate the legitimate offers from the fakes. In the end a legitimate offer of $5,001 took home the test showing that the pop diva was with child. Money raised from the auction went to support two charities, Candlelighters Childhood Cancer Foundation and the Easter Seals Society. There was no word on whether or not DNA testing was planned to confirm the item's authenticity.

THE BEER CUP THAT LAUNCHED A THOUSAND FISTS

It was called by many the worst brawl in NBA history and, perhaps, the worst that has ever taken place in professional sports. With 45.9 seconds left in a game between the Indiana Pacers and the Detroit Pistons, a hard foul occurred. At first the fight that ensued seemed like nothing more than your run-of-the-mill on-court argument. There was some pushing and shoving but tempers were cooling and the referees appeared to have the situation under control.

That is, until a Piston fan threw a beer cup at Indiana Pacer star Ron Artest, who had removed himself from the commotion and was seated near the scorer's table. What happened next was played over and over again on network television for days. In short, Artest jumped into the stands to go after the man whom he believed threw the cup, fans and players began swinging at one another, and the brawl took on a life of its own. In the end, there were multiple arrests of players and fans and the harshest punishments ever handed down in professional basketball for fighting.

Shortly after the brawl ended, what was said to be the cup that had started it all appeared on eBay. Called a "must-have collectible for all Ron Artest fans," the cup resembled thousands of others sold during that and prior Detroit Piston home games. Bidding went out of control and less than twenty-four hours later the auction was pulled despite its 109 bids and a high bid of $99 million.

Following this first cup offered on eBay were dozens like it. Since there was no way to distinguish the true cup from the pretenders, eBay was forced to round up all the cups and pull them from the site.

Also listed for sale were popcorn containers said to be the same ones thrown in the general direction of the brawlers. After the dust cleared, beer cups and popcorn containers were allowed to remain on eBay as long as claims were not made about their being the ones shown on television. Multiple empty cups and containers from Piston games sold for far in excess of what they would have cost to purchase full at a game. Why someone would want to purchase these discarded plastic and cardboard containers is another question entirely.

WOULD YOU LIKE SYRUP WITH YOUR FRENCH TOAST?

At the turn of the year 2000 the world breathed a sigh of re-lief when computers everywhere did not crash because of the Y2K bug. George Bush and Al Gore clashed in an epic presidential race. The boy band *NSYNC ruled the hearts and minds of teenyboppers around the world. Justin Timberlake was perhaps the most well-known member of the group, and his celebrated relationship with fellow teen superstar Britney Spears was the hot topic of celebrity gossip columns everywhere. The year 2000 was also the year Timberlake did an interview with New York radio station Z100 and failed to finish his French toast.

Up for auction on March 9, the same afternoon as the interview, went eBay item 279562051, "JUSTIN TIMBERLAKE'S FRENCH TOAST **Z100**." According to the description of the item, the entire *NSYNC band had been on Z100 earlier that morning and, amazingly, Timberlake had eaten only one bite of the French toast he was served. The lucky high bidder was promised this toast "complete with extra syrup," the fork he used, and the plate upon which the infamous piece of toast was served.

Although the item was put up before visitor counters were a regular eBay feature, the auction was spotlighted in news stories around the world and the attention it received rivaled the most well-known eBay auctions of the time. In total, 40 bids were received and the French toast sold for an astounding $3,154. Z100 stipulated that it would be verifying all bids received in excess of $1,000, and although the seller was never identified, the sale reportedly went through. According to the description of the auction, all money raised by the sale went to a Z100-supported charity.

THE BECKHAM BALL

In the United Kingdom David Beckham is as close to royalty as one can get without being born a prince or princess. As captain of England's soccer team he is the idol of millions, and as husband to Posh Spice he is a constant target of the paparazzi. When his country's team met Portugal's in the Euro 2004 quarterfinal, all of England's hopes for a European soccer championship rode on the shoulders of the game's most famous face. After a grueling regulation and overtime left the match tied at 2–2, the contest moved toward climax in a dramatic penalty shoot-out. All of Europe held its breath as England's captain and star stepped up to take the first shot for his country.

From only twelve yards away from goal the advantage lies with the shooter, but as Beckham approached the ball he slipped slightly, and his shot sailed high of the goal and into the stands. England lost the shoot-out and the match 6–5. He went home the goat of the game. As for the ball, it landed in the lap of Pablo Carral, a Spanish fan, sitting in row Q. Carral declined an initial offer of 18,000 euros (US$22,685) for the ball and, instead, the trophy popped up as item number 3688276550 on eBay Spain.

Bidding and interest in the ball were intense, and for a time the price reached more than $12 million. After measures were put in place to screen out bogus bids, the ball sold for the more reasonable price of approximately $35,000. The winning bidder was none other than GoldenPalace.com, and the company quickly found a good use for the infamous purchase. The soccer relic now travels the world raising money for charity: willing donors get a shot to do what Beckham could not—kick the famous ball into the goal from the penalty stripe of a local soccer field.

BLACK BETSY

The legend of Shoeless Joe Jackson and his bat "Black Betsy" is as familiar to baseball fans as the story of King Arthur and his sword Excalibur is to history aficionados. Shoeless Joe Jackson was considered one of baseball's greatest players in the early part of the twentieth century, and he credited much of this success on the playing field to his bat, Black Betsy.

Legend had it that Black Betsy somehow remained serviceable throughout the ballplayer's entire career. Over the years, however, knowledge of the bat's whereabouts was lost and it became a myth. It was the subject of tall tales and the occasional book, but there were few who believed the bat truly existed. That was until 2001 when, miraculously, it turned up on eBay.

Between the time it was last used by Jackson and the time it appeared on eBay, the bat mostly sat anonymously on Lester Erwin's bookshelf in Easley, South Carolina. Erwin had inherited the bat in 1959 from Shoeless Joe Jackson's widow, a cousin of Erwin's mother. Apparently he was unaware of the bat's true value or its significance to legions of fans who still speak of it in hushed tones.

The auction of Black Betsy began July 26, 2001, with a required deposit of $25,000 in order to limit bogus bids. Although thousands of baseball fans and curious eBayers visited the auction during its ten-day run and dozens of people ponied up the required $25,000, only two people actually bid. The lack of bids probably reflected the incredible value of the artifact, and not a lack of interest in the collectible.

When the auction ended on August 6, the final price was an astounding $577,610. The winning bid was cast by Rob Mitchell, a thirty-year-old owner of a marketing company in Pottstown, Pennsylvania. He planned to display the bat in his company's office.

PROBABLY NOT FIT TO DRINK

In 2002, Christina Aguilera did a photo shoot for *Maxim* in which she was required to wear a thong and pose partially submerged in a bathtub full of water. The pictures appeared in a spread in the January 2003 issue of the magazine. It was a little more than a year before a vial of the bathwater she had soaked in and the thong she had worn that day showed up on eBay.

Item number 2594748875, titled "Christina Aguilera's Thong and Pool Water," went live on UK eBay on February 11, 2004. The seller assured potential customers he had obtained the collectibles legally in a radio contest conducted by Scott Mills of the BBC. Mills reportedly acquired the items from a source at *Maxim*.

The lucky winner of the auction was entitled to, among other things, the thong, a sealed tube of water, and a signed note from Mills stating, "Enjoy drinking from the cup as much as I did." The auction recorded hundreds of thousands of views and at the height of its fame attracted more than 60,000 looks in one day. The final price for the one-of-a-kind Aguilera collectibles? $1,535.

PATSY'S PLANE

Patsy Cline remains one of country music's most influential performers. She began her recording career in the mid-1950s and by the early 1960s was one of country music's biggest stars. On March 5, 1963, the thirty-year-old singer was killed when her plane crashed in Camden, Tennessee. More than thirty-five years later, wreckage from this accident appeared on eBay.

The auction began on September 1, 2001, with an opening asking price of $50,000. The sale was conducted by a set of brothers who were offering a portion of the plane's belly and tail that they obtained from their father and another family. The items were well documented and there was no real question surrounding their authenticity.

By September 6, the auction had been bid up to $50,100 when eBay canceled the sale. According to an article in *USA Today*, eBay spokesperson Kevin Purslove said, "The auction was most likely taken down as the result of an eBay policy dealing with items related to horrific events, accidents and murders." EBay, after consulting with the brothers, ultimately relented and allowed the auction to be resubmitted.

Many Patsy Cline fans were "up in arms" about the sale before the first auction was even begun, and then 9/11 happened in the midst of the second sale. So it should come as little surprise that no buyers materialized during the auction's second iteration. Despite threatening legal action against eBay for removing the items, the sellers never formally filed complaints, and it is rumored the plane parts were sold privately.

JAY LENO'S HOG

A month after the terrorist attacks of 9/11, Jay Leno wanted to do something to help the victims. He came up with the idea of auctioning off one of the motorcycles from his legendary car and motorcycle collection.

Up for sale in October of 2001 went a Harley Davidson FXDL Dyna Low Rider that Leno had purchased the previous July. Among the bike's main selling points were its low mileage (only 200 miles) and a custom black leather seat. As an added bonus, Jay had arranged for more than two dozen of his celebrity guests to sign the bike. Among those who put their John Hancock on the Harley were Sylvester Stallone, Denzel Washington, Nicole Kidman, John Travolta, Nicolas Cage, Cuba Gooding Jr., Pamela Anderson, Magic Johnson, Mira Sorvino, Terry Bradshaw, Tom Cruise, and Arnold Schwarzenegger.

After ten days on eBay the sale ended with a winning bid of $360,200 from a New Mexico water driller named Frank Davis. Davis took possession of the bike during an airing of *The Tonight Show* and said he planned to raise more money with the bike.

When the tsunami struck Indonesia in December of 2004, a second Harley appeared on Jay Leno's show. Harley Davidson and the West Coast Harley dealership BartelsHarley donated a 2005 FLHR Road King bike, and this time more than sixty celebrities penned their names on the hog. When it was put up on eBay, a total of 219 bids were received. The winning bidder was David P. Stenier of Waste Management Inc., who agreed to pay $800,100 for the one-of-a-kind Harley. The proceeds from the ten-day auction benefited Red Cross International disaster relief efforts.

Following the auction, the bike took a road trip around the United States as part of an effort to raise more money for the relief effort. Among its stops was a weeklong stay in former president Clinton's presidential museum in Little Rock, Arkansas.

AN END TO THE CURSE

In 1918 the Boston Red Sox won their fifth World Series. It was the most by any team at that time and the Red Sox were baseball's premier club. On this 1918 championship team was a young pitcher named Babe Ruth. Ruth was a rising star, and Red Sox fans hoped the young man would help deliver many more championships. But in 1919 Red Sox owner Harry Frazee reportedly needed money to help finance his relationship with a girlfriend, so Ruth was sold to the hated New York Yankees in the winter after the 1919 season for $100,000.

The rest is history. Ruth became perhaps the most famous player of all time, and the Yankees, who until then had never won a championship, went on to become baseball's most storied franchise, with twenty-six World Series titles. As for the Red Sox, the team would not win another championship for eighty-six years. At some point in this stretch, Red Sox fans began to blame the drought on the sale of Ruth, and thus was born the "Curse of the Bambino."

In 2004 the Red Sox finally broke their winless streak with a World Series sweep over the St. Louis Cardinals. Following this improbable championship run, up for sale on eBay went item number 5135174066, titled "1919 Original Babe Ruth Sale Contract." This was the very contract between Frazee and his counterpart, Yankee owner Jacob Ruppert, that brought Ruth to the Yankees on December 26, 1919.

The eBay auction of the famous contract began on October 30, 2004, with an opening bid of $50,000 and ran for ten days. The owner of the contract, philanthropist Alan Shawn Feinstein, had purchased it for $99,000 in 1993, and he promised that all money from the sale would go to charity. Yet despite intense media attention, hundreds of thousands of visits to the site, and 206 bids, the final sale price of $470,100 fell short of the reserve placed on the auction and the item did not change hands through eBay. A second auction held by Sotheby's in June of 2005, also for charity, resulted in the sale of the contract for $996,000 to a die-hard Yankees fan.

A DRINK FIT FOR THE KING

Elvis Presley passed away long before eBay was even a gleam in eBay founder Pierre Omidyar's eye. Although items somehow related to Presley are a staple on eBay, one has to wonder how much a half-eaten peanut butter and banana sandwich, the King's legendary favorite, would have drawn had eBay been around while he was devouring them. We may never know the answer to that question, but if auction 3861592313 is any indication, such a sale certainly would generate quite a bit of media attention.

The auction item was described as "a sealed glass bottle with water from Elvis's cup that he drank [from] while onstage in Charlotte, NC 2/12/1977." According to the seller, he was thirteen years old when he obtained the cup at one of the King's final concerts. After the show was over the seller was seeking a souvenir and the security guard gave him the cup Elvis had drunk from during the concert. The young man stored the water and the cup in a freezer until 1988, when he transferred the water into a glass vial.

Inspired by the $28,000 sale of the Virgin Mary grilled

cheese sandwich featured on eBay the month before, after squirreling away his treasure for twenty-eight years in his icebox, the seller decided to see what he could get for the water on eBay. While interest in the auction was significant, apparently a higher value was attached to the actual cup. The final sale price for the vial of water was only $455, but offers flooded in asking to purchase the cup.

Although the seller refused all offers to outright sell the foam container from which the King had slurped, the seller did put up a second auction that would entitle the winner to take the cup on tour. This auction ended early when the cookie company Nutballz agreed to pay an undisclosed sum for the privilege of borrowing it. The company brought the cup and its owner to Colorado, where they conducted a fund-raiser that benefited the Center for Celiac Research.

YOUR NAME IN LIGHTS!

Romeo and Juliet, Ebenezer Scrooge, Captain Ahab, Sherlock Holmes. These are just a few of the most famous fictional characters ever created. But how did Shakespeare, Dickens, and the rest decide that these names should be given to their creations? The world may never know, but one thing these famous authors certainly did not do was turn to eBay and allow the high bidder to name a character after him- or herself. Yet in the fall of 2005 some of the most well-known contemporary writers did exactly that.

Beginning September 1, 2005, eighteen separate auctions offered fans the opportunity to bid to have their name used in upcoming works of fiction being written by their favorite authors. Among the writers participating in the charity auctions were Stephen King, John Grisham, Amy Tan, and Lemony Snicket. The details of each auction differed slightly from sale to sale. For instance, in auction number 6559998991 Stephen King warned, "Buyer should be aware *Cell* is a violent piece of work which comes complete with zombies set in motion by bad cell phone signals that destroy the human brain. . . . Character can be male or female but a buyer who wants to die must in this case be female." David Brin, on the other hand, offered the high bidder in auction number 6561889065 the opportunity for "something original. Let the winning bidder choose between the name of a rogue moon on a collision course with an unnamed planet, an exotic and gruesome disease of unknown origin or an entire species of wise, ancient extraterrestrials."

Auctions ran for ten days and were staggered throughout the month of September. The auction granting the winner the opportunity to have a character named after him or her in the upcoming Stephen King book drew the highest bid of the bunch, $25,100. This was followed by the auction for a character's name in John Grisham's upcoming book, with the winner forking over $12,100. For the more cost-conscious shopper, naming rights of a character in a forthcoming ZZ Packer book were had for only $520.

In total the auctions were viewed by 105,000 people and attracted 674 bids. All money raised by the eighteen sales, $81,817 in total, went to benefit the First Amendment Project, which is a nonprofit organization "dedicated to protecting and promoting freedom of information, expression and petition."

Believe in What You Sell

I t is a textbook lesson in the art of successful selling; sell a product you believe in. If you do not have faith in the merchandise you are trying to push, how can you expect to generate interest and top dollar for whatever it is you have to offer?

The case studies in this lesson are dedicated to examining the ways in which people's beliefs lead directly to higher sale prices and more media attention. If the woman who sold her half-eaten grilled cheese sandwich had not truly believed that the Virgin Mary had miraculously appeared on her lunch, would the auction have generated the level of publicity that it did? More to the point, would a nonbeliever have even noticed the Virgin Mary to begin with, or posted the sandwich for sale rather than taking those last, few, delicious bites?

Be on the lookout for miracles, because they can appear anywhere. As the case studies in this chapter show, miracles can be found in things as seemingly ordinary as a bag of pretzels. Also, you would be wise to be on the lookout for images appearing in stains near your bathroom shower.

You must also remember to remain true to your beliefs no matter what comments you may receive from fellow eBayers. If the man who sold the time machine that did not work had begun doubting the nature of his offering because a couple of malicious individuals called him crazy, would he have become famous for his auction? Of course not. As you work to create the next notorious eBay sale, take care to find an item you truly believe in and you could make it and yourself a star.

HOW MUCH FOR THAT HALF-EATEN GRILLED CHEESE?

It is not the sort of question one typically ponders: How much could I get for this half-eaten grilled cheese sandwich? Yet in November of 2004 that is exactly what a seller from Fort Lauderdale, Florida, put up for sale on eBay. Of course, it helps if your grilled cheese seems to contain an image of the Virgin Mary and possesses magical powers.

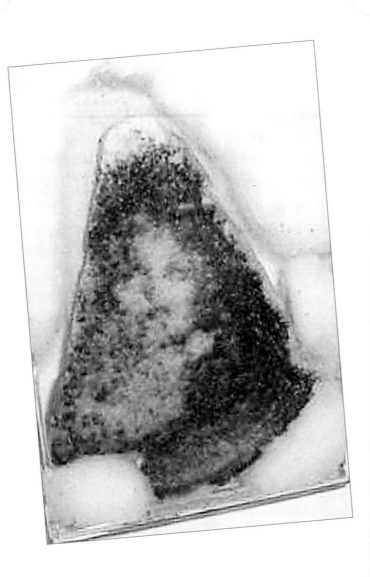

According to the auction ad, the seller had made the sandwich a decade ago and, "when I took a bite out of it I saw a face looking up at me. It was the Virgin Mary staring back at me." The seller goes on to point out that the grilled cheese sandwich had not been preserved in any way over the years, and that since making the sandwich she had won $70,000 on different occasions at casinos near her home. The seller believed her incredible good luck was evidence of the sandwich's divine power. Further, she said that she "would like all people to know that I do believe this is the Virgin Mary, Mother of God."

The sandwich was first put up for sale in early November and generated an initial wave of publicity. EBay pulled the auction because, according to CNN, as the company explained in an email to the seller, eBay "does not allow listings that are intended as jokes."

But it was no joke, and when, with just hours before the auction was set to close, with bidding at $22,000, eBay pulled the item, the seller, identified as Diana Duyser, complained to the media, "How could eBay do this to me?" She then petitioned eBay, convinced them she was not joking, that she truly believed in her sandwich, and the company eventually relented.

The item was relisted, and eBay helped Duyser pre-screen her bidders to decide which ones were legitimate. Whereas the first auction was viewed by slightly more than 80,000 people, the relisted item attracted many millions of views before closing on November 22, 2004.

During the second auction, bidding began at $3,000

and attracted 27 bids on the way to a final sale price of $28,000. The winning bidder? GoldenPalace.com. It is too early to tell whether or not the sandwich has made the casino's gamblers luckier or vice versa, but, according to the company's CEO Richard Rowe, the casino plans on using the famous grilled cheese sandwich to raise money for charity.

In the early summer of 2005 the creator of the holy sandwich turned to eBay once again to auction off the frying pan that created the grilled cheese Madonna. After a five-day sale, GoldenPalace.com added the sandwich's maker, auction number 5577372276, to its collection for $5,999.99.

JESUS OF THE BATHROOM WALL

If the Virgin Mary could be found in a grilled cheese sandwich then it should come as no surprise that Jesus was spotted in a plaster wall next to a bathroom shower just outside of Pittsburgh, Pennsylvania. Item 6186339869 went live on June 11, 2005, and was titled "Jesus Christ Image Icon Materializes in Plaster Wall."

According to the seller, he first noticed the image when he stepped out of the shower on June 11. He was also quick to try to relieve skeptics of any doubts they might have about his sale, saying at the outset that the wall had not been doctored and that the photos he posted on eBay had not been staged. The seller declined all requests to speak with radio shows, going so far as to add a line to his auction description stating that he would not do radio interviews because "interviews make Baby Jebus cry."

As interest in the relic intensified, the seller required that potential bidders register in advance of bidding. This measure kept the auction from being overwhelmed by hoax bidders, but it probably also served to keep the relic from soaring in value, as fake bids tend to push interested parties into bidding higher than they otherwise would have to. Despite more than 125,000 visits, the item received only one bid and sold for the initial asking price of $1,999.99. The proceeds should be enough for the seller to at least repair the hole in the wall the removal of the plaster caused.

Perhaps coincidentally, the bathroom wall image of Jesus was discovered just a few hundred miles from Chicago where, in the spring of 2005, believers made worldwide headlines by erecting a shrine to a water stain bearing the image of Jesus that had appeared on an underpass of the Dan Ryan Expressway. Given the time and distance between the two appearances, one might advance the argument that Jesus was walking east across the upper Midwest during the spring of 2005.

THE MEANING OF LIFE

It is a question everyone at one point or another ponders: what is the meaning of life? It is often said in response that there are no easy answers to this question, but to one lucky eBayer, that was decidedly not the case. Put up for sale on January 29, 2000, item 248619068 was titled simply "The Meaning of Life."

The description of the item was short and to the point. It consisted of only one line: "I have discovered the reason for our existence and will be happy to share this information with the highest bidder." The seller had accumulated more than 200 positive feedback comments and offered this seemingly priceless piece of information for a starting bid of just one penny. Despite its obvious value, the item attracted only 8 offers and the auction closed with a sale price of just $3.26.

Although the item did not attract much media attention during its short life on eBay, after the sale closed news of the auction began circulating through the Internet and attracting sarcastic jokes about how cheaply such knowledge had been bought. The auction ultimately has since been mentioned in numerous articles written on a range of topics.

The seller reports that he has received countless emails over the years from others requesting the knowledge he possesses—"enough to start a cult," he said. He responds to all of them that he is sorry "but I sold the meaning of life and I don't have the rights to it anymore." He also stated that although he was not asked, he refunded the buyer's money when the buyer sought more guidance after the initial answer was provided.

THE HAUNTED PAINTING

The auction for item 251789217 was titled simply "Haunted Painting—Warning and Disclaimer," and it made its debut appearance on eBay on February 2, 2000. The painting shows two young children standing in front of a window in an eerie state of animation. But it was not the painting, in and of itself, that attracted thousands of viewers to

the auction. Instead, it was the description and the seller's claims about the haunting piece of art that sparked a fascination that has caused the item, even today, to remain a regular subject of discussion on paranormal Web sites and discussion boards.

According to the individual who offered the item for sale, the painting had been found abandoned behind an old brewery in California. After the seller took the painting home, strange occurrences began. Among other things, the seller claimed her four-and-a-half-year-old daughter came into her bedroom one evening and said that the children in the painting "were fighting and coming into the room at night." After setting up a motion-activated camera, the seller apparently obtained photos that seem to show the boy exiting the picture. These photos were included on the auction page. The seller's description and the debate the painting generated pushed the price of the item from an opening asking price of $199 to $1,095.

Since the sale, "Haunted Painting" has been identified as a work called *The Hands Resist Him* created by artist Bill Stoneham in 1972. Today the artist has capitalized on the fame of the auction and made available prints of the picture, along with its story, through his Stoneham Studios Web site, www.stonehamstudios.com.

The artist claims on his Web page that the painting is not haunted and that he used himself as a model for the boy in the picture. His assurances, however, have not quelled debate. Stoneham also states on his Web site that he has no idea what happened to the actor who originally purchased the painting or how it came to be abandoned in the old building. There is little question that the current owner of the painting would be able to make a small fortune should he or she decide to relist the now infamous piece of art on eBay.

GRANDPA'S GHOST

Auction 5539709069 came about because of a young child's fear of ghosts. Or, rather, the fear of one ghost in particular: that of his recently deceased grandfather. Titled "Ghost Cane Free shipping!" the auction went live November 29, 2004, and the description began, "My 5-year-old son believes the ghost of my father haunts our house (which was once my father's house)."

Apparently the grandfather at the center of this story was battling lung cancer in 2003 and, at times, would become frustrated with his young grandson who could not understand what was happening. When his grandfather passed away, the child became convinced that his grandfather's malevolent spirit still haunted the house, and the child asked his mother to sell the old man's spirit on eBay. The child's mother, eager to appease her worried child, obliged. To ensure that someone received the ghost, the child asked that his grandfather's cane be included with the auction. The seller promised she would buy something special for the child with the proceeds.

Little did the seller know the power of eBay. First local and then national media got wind of the story and the seller and her auction were featured on every major network in the country. The seller appeared overwhelmed by the responses and, in the midst of the sale, added the following comment to her auction: "Please don't go overboard on this. I just want to make my son feel at ease here . . . I am a nervous wreck right now. I can't believe this went so far. Please keep the bidding at a minimum."

Despite being perhaps the only seller in history to tell people not to bid on her item, the ghost and accompanying cane sold for $65,100. It just goes to show that eBay can solve your problems and make you rich.

GHOST IN A JAR

The title begged for further clarification: "Ghost in a Jar! No Joke Serious Inquiry Only." Listed on May 27, 2003, auction number 2931457201 became one of the most heavily viewed items ever listed on eBay.

In the description of the item the vendor began by telling the world he had come across the Ghost in a Jar when he was out metal-detecting nearly two decades ago in an abandoned cemetery. While digging, about two feet down his shovel struck a rotting wooden box. "There were

2 jars and an old journal in the box," he started. "The jars had some strange writing and symbols on them. While getting the jars out of the ground I dropped one and it broke. A black mist seeped out. . . ."

The seller went on to detail his haunting by "The Black Thing," which was apparently unleashed when the jar was broken. He said that this "Black Thing" had twice attacked him and seemed bent on causing him physical harm. After discussing his situation with someone who was "versed in these things," the seller determined the only way he was going to be rid of the haunting was to pass on the second, unopened, jar to someone else.

By all indications the seller seemed to seriously believe in the item he was selling. He posted numerous responses to the deluge of email he received and repeatedly stated that this was not a hoax. He also told those who wrote him that he had tried to dispose of the Ghost in a Jar by reburying it, but this effort only caused the "Black Thing" to become more active.

By the time the auction finally ended it had garnered worldwide publicity, attracted millions of viewers, and the price of the Ghost in a Jar had climbed from the original opening bid of $99 to $50,922. These figures do not reflect several fake bids that, at times, pushed the asking price to as high a figure as eBay can record: $99,999,999.

For bidders who could not afford the original thing, hundreds of copycat auctions for other ghosts in jars or knockoffs, such as "Ghost in a Bra," "Ghost in a Wine Bottle for Those Afraid of Jars," and "Homeless Ghost

Looking for a Jar," became available. If you missed out on this original wave of activity, not to worry. It is the rare day that passes when a Ghost in a Jar is not listed for sale on eBay, although the prices on these items have dropped significantly.

THE LORD WORKS IN MYSTERIOUS WAYS

It came from a bag of Rold Gold Honey Mustard Tiny Twist Pretzels and, according to the description of item 6158640078, it was found by a twelve-year-old girl in St. Paul, Nebraska, on February 27, 2005. The sellers of the item claimed that a feeling of warmth and spirituality possessed them when they held the pretzel.

Measuring roughly one inch by two inches, to the untrained eye it looked like little more than an oddly shaped pretzel. According to *USA Today*, the seventh-grader who found the pretzel initially thought it looked like an *S*, but when she showed it to her mom, her mom believed it looked like the Virgin Mary holding Baby Jesus—as did many thousands of people world-wide. Fortunately the young girl consulted her mother and did not consume the tasty relic.

With help from mentions on numerous television programs including the *Tony Danza Show*, the auction generated 79,428 views during its ten-day run on eBay and attracted 56 bids. Although bidding at one point reached $15,000, after screening measures were implemented to regulate the bidding process, the item was scooped up for a mere $10,600.

Despite initially planning to use the proceeds to purchase a horse, the sellers decided during the course of the auction to instead donate the money to their two churches. For the record, a bag of Rold Gold Honey Mustard Tiny Twist Pretzels retails for about $3.29.

RISKING THE WRATH OF GOD

When Pope John Paul II passed away, eBay was flooded with items that were in some way associated with the former pontiff. While most of these auctions raised little attention, item 6169851381 and a subsequent one, item 6171703649, drew media condemnation from around the world and resulted in a change in eBay policies. The controversy? Two different sellers put up for sale a Eucharistic wafer allegedly consecrated by the pope. To Catholics the celebration of the Eucharist is a central sacrament of the Church, and the consecrated Host is believed to be literally the Body of Christ.

The seller of the first consecrated Host stated he was not a Catholic and does "not believe I'm going to hell for selling this collectible." According to the seller, he obtained the wafer at a Mass in Rome on October 18, 1998.

Outraged that someone would sell the consecrated Host, Catholic groups from around the world began denouncing eBay in letters that poured into the company.

Throughout the auction, eBay said that it would not remove the item because it was not illegal to sell the wafer, and that while some might find the auction distasteful, it did not violate any company policy. Ultimately the wafer sold for $2,000 to a devout Catholic who made the purchase to keep the wafer from being "desecrated further." After the sale ended, however, the seller reportedly agreed to turn the wafer over to the archbishop of Iowa City and no money ever changed hands.

When the auction appeared for the second wafer reportedly consecrated by Pope John Paul II, similar protests were logged with eBay and the company finally relented and removed the item. EBay also sent a letter of apology to Catholic representatives who had protested the sale. The company vowed it would remove similar items in the future.

HOLY ROLLER

For sale: eBay Germany listing 4545301886. A 1999 gray Volkswagen Golf hatchback. 47,000 miles, in good condition. Oh, and one other thing, it used to belong to Cardinal Ratzinger before he was elevated to Pope Benedict XVI.

When twenty-one-year-old Benjamin Halbe from the small German town of Olpe bought a 1999 Volkswagen Golf hatchback in January 2005, he paid about $12,500. At the time, Pope John Paul II was still alive and Cardinal Joseph Ratzinger was an influential but relatively little-known world figure. The cardinal had recently, through his secretary, sold his used '99 Volkswagen to a car dealership in Olpe. After Cardinal Ratzinger became pope, Benjamin Halbe went back to look at his registration and confirmed that he was indeed the owner of the new pope's old car.

When the car was posted for sale on eBay Germany, the attention it drew was like none the auction site in that country had ever seen. More than eight and a half million people visited the page while it was live, and journalists from around the world ran stories on the "holy ride."

When the bidding ended, GoldenPalace.com came away as the auction's victor. The final sale price was $245,000, with both the number of views for an auction and the final sale price setting records for eBay Germany. GoldenPalace .com has announced that the car will be going on an extended worldwide road trip visiting towns and cities nominated by visitors to their Web site.

THE ANTI-POPE MOBILE

While some of those eBayers who were interested in the car that once belonged to the current pope probably think there is something spiritual about the car, one has to wonder what they would think about item 4551210578. It was another car that had belonged to a celebrity, although probably no one would be willing to claim that this automobile had the same type of spiritual aura surrounding it.

The auction title read simply "2004 Cadillac Escalade," but if you went in for a closer look you would have found that the eighteen-foot limousine had been custom-built for shock jock Howard Stern. The car was first put up for sale May 19, 2005, by the man known to Howard Stern fans as "Ronnie the Limo Driver." The vehicle, the description claimed, had been driven less than 15,000 miles and had been signed by Howard Stern himself. It would be presented to the winning bidder in a special ceremony.

Perhaps put off by Stern's constant references to how much he hated the car, Ronnie the Limo Driver had a difficult time selling the Escalade. The first time it went up on the block the auction failed to generate a legitimate bid despite 61,337 views. The opening bid was $89,000, but this amount still would not have met the reserve. Immediately following the close of the first unsuccessful sale attempt, the car went back up on eBay, with a lower opening bid. This time, despite 81,388 page views, bidding petered out at $64,200 and again failed to meet the reserve set by the seller. A third attempt to sell the car generated only 3,962 page views, and once again the car failed to sell.

Stupid Criminals Have a Place on EBay Too

As we shall see in the following pages, a criminal act exposed over eBay may get a person some real media notoriety, but it's probably not the kind of notoriety most good eBayers crave. Flogging your lawlessness on eBay might make you famous, but how much enjoyment can you derive from name recognition while you're doing time in jail?

As the case studies in this lesson highlight, there is something about eBay that attracts the most trusting of criminals. For some reason criminals tend to think if they post an item that is illegal to sell, only those interested in the item and not those intent on arresting them will take notice of their auction. Perhaps it is a general belief among criminals that law enforcement officers are behind the times in terms of technological sophistication, or perhaps the criminally inclined simply lack an understanding of just how visible eBay auctions can become. If you choose this tactic, you'll want to make sure to cover your tracks well.

Just because you attempt to commit a felony through eBay does not guarantee you will become an Internet celebrity. The recipes others have used to successfully distinguish their criminal acts vary dramatically. Posting auctions with pictures actually showing yourself surrounded by large quantities of narcotics is likely to get you noticed. Failing spectacularly when committing a criminal act is also a sure ticket to fame.

For the record, selling drugs, selling people into slavery, and stealing property are still illegal even if you deliver on your sale and receive positive feedback from a happy eBay customer.

PERHAPS NOBODY WILL MISS IT

Two days after the debacle that was the 2000 presidential election, the nation looked on as those in Palm Beach County, Florida, counted and recounted butterfly ballots and made judgments on hanging chads. Meanwhile, two Floridians got the bright idea that the infamous ballot boxes might be something someone somewhere would be willing to pay a lot of money for. So they stole one. And then they listed it on eBay.

Although it can be argued that recognizing the "collectible" nature of an otherwise useless ballot box requires some degree of intelligence, putting a stolen one up for sale in an extremely visible, public forum with the whole world watching earned these would-be auctioneers a dubious place among the most infamous of eBay criminals. After being tipped off by an election official who saw the auction, Palm Beach County law enforcement officers made contact with the sellers, pretending to be interested in purchasing the item. The asking price for the box was originally $2,000 but the sellers upped their desired commission to $20,000 after being contacted by the officers. The pair were in jail well before the presidential election had been officially decided.

Perhaps taking a cue from these misguided criminals, Palm Beach County created a bit of a stir with its own noteworthy eBay auctions. In late 2001, the county decided to sell off the infamous voting machine, butterfly ballots, and ballot boxes on eBay. For $300 a buyer received one of 560 voting machines and a supply of ballots. For another $300 ($600 total) an individual could also get his or her very own ballot box.

YOU MEAN TRAFFICKING IN HUMAN BEINGS
IS FROWNED UPON?

On March 2, 2004, one of the most disturbing auctions ever submitted to eBay went live on eBay's Taiwan site. The description was sparse in nature but, according to Rachel Konrad of the Associated Press, "The site included five photos of three people. One dark-haired woman in a white shirt wore makeup and blue nail polish, and the other two appeared to be girls no older than their early teens." The auction had an opening bid of 180,000 Taiwanese dollars (US$5,400) and remained live for at least three days until it was brought to the attention of eBay and removed.

In the description the seller never, outside of the photos, actually made reference to what was being sold, saying simply that the "goods" were made in Vietnam and would be shipped to Thailand only. The ambiguity of this sparse description only made the auction more suspicious to some, and, while eBay pulled the item, suspended the user, and turned the contact information he or she provided over to local authorities, there has been no word since on the individual responsible for the auction. It is widely assumed he or she was never located.

The one good that did come from this auction was that attention was directed to the illegal trade in young women and girls who are forced to work in the sex industry. Newspapers from all over the world published the story, emphasizing how prevalent human trafficking continues to be in some parts of the world.

THE PRICE OF DOING BUSINESS

In the United States this auction probably would have generated little publicity. But the item was put up for sale on Baazee.com, the eBay-owned commerce site in India, and it resulted in the arrest of eBay India's number one executive, American Avnish Bajaj, for peddling pornography.

The controversy began in December 2004 when an Indian student offered for sale a homemade two-minute video clip of two seventeen-year-old high school students engaging in sexual acts. The clip had been created by the two students on one of their mobile phones. When the couple broke up, the video clip began circulating around India after one of the teenagers sent it to friends. The seller had obtained a copy of the footage and placed it for sale in the books and magazines section of Baazee.com. Eight copies of the clip were sold at $3 apiece.

Although the clip was never shown on the site and the company removed the offending item as soon as it became aware of the situation, Indian officials claim that the sale violated the country's Information Technology Act, which regulates the sale of online pornography. Baazee's chief went to New Delhi to help police with their investigation only to be arrested himself. EBay issued a strong statement condemning the arrest, and Condoleezza Rice involved the U.S. government, demanding the accused U.S. citizen be given a fair trial. Eventually Bajaj was granted bail and asked not to leave the country until the investigation was completed. To date, no further charges have been leveled against Bajaj.

NEITHER RAIN, NOR SLEET, NOR SNOW, BUT WHAT ABOUT EBAY?

If you sent a package to Berlin between the summer of 2003 and April of 2004 and it never arrived, you might have been successful locating it on eBay. The reason? Apparently a German postal carrier decided to supplement his income by absconding with packages he was supposed to deliver and selling the contents online.

According to Berlin police, the thefts of more than one hundred items with an estimated value of $23,700 have been linked to the postal carrier. The man did little to hide his identity. German authorities were tipped off when they heard from a musician that a clarinet mouthpiece he expected to receive by mail never arrived. The musician had subsequently found an identical item on eBay Germany and alerted the police. The musician, perhaps to be sure he finally got the needed mouthpiece, also bid on the item and won.

The postal employee allegedly admitted to the thefts after a search of his apartment turned up more missing packages. Apparently the postal carrier had no problem delivering his stolen wares to his buyers, since there were no recorded complaints logged against the seller for failure to deliver purchases consummated on eBay. While there have been several other cases throughout the years in which stolen mail items have appeared on eBay, this is the first and only known case in which the perpetrator was the person charged with delivering the items.

WHY SURGEONS SOMETIMES OPERATE ON THE WRONG LEG

The American Board of Surgery is responsible for administering examinations to doctors seeking certification to perform surgery. The Board's 290-question exams determine whether or not doctors can actually go ahead and perform the surgeries that they have been studying in medical school and residencies for years. When one rectal specialist from Florida failed the exam in 2002, he flew to Philadelphia to review his results. While there he also took the opportunity to copy down the questions and then hawked them along with the answers on eBay.

According to the auction listing on eBay, "These are the actual certifying general surgery board questions with correct answers, guaranteed to improve your test score." Although the original auctions did not receive significant attention at the time of their listings, they did come to the attention of the American Board of Surgery, which made contact with the seller through a couple of anonymous emails.

While news stories of high school and college students seeking to cheat on SAT or graduate school exams such as the GMAT or LSAT are fairly common, this story was unique. Once the press was made aware of it, the rectal specialist found his name plastered all over the news.

According to the surgeon's lawyer, the doctor sold "two or three sets of questions for $180 to $300," which was, in retrospect, a very bad business decision. In addition to damaging his practice, losing his certification (he'd passed the exam on his next attempt in 2003), and having to pay the lawyer's fees, the doctor also was ordered to pay $36,000 to the American Board of Surgery. This was the estimated cost to get the experts together to develop a new set of questions for future exams. Thanks to one rectal specialist, the policy of allowing doctors to see their results in private for a $100 fee has been discontinued.

THE DEA HAS COMPUTERS TOO

The auction lasted only twenty-one hours but it certainly ranks high among the most famous of eBay sales. In an auction listed on September 21, 1999, the sellers claimed to be offering five hundred pounds of marijuana. The ad stated that the auctioneers were selling "Holland's best," and pictures posted with the sale featured three men posing with many, many bags of what appeared to be marijuana.

Twenty-one hours later, eBay shut down the auction, but not before the story broke in papers around the world and the item had recorded seven bids, pushing the price to $10 million. For those keeping track, that is $1,250 an ounce.

EBay had immediately notified the DEA, which responded that it would aggressively pursue an investigation into the listing. No arrests were ever announced.

Because of the photographs included with the auction, the marijuana sale is probably the most well-known auction for illegal drugs that has taken place on eBay, but several other similar auctions have also made news. Just a couple of months before the five hundred pounds of pot went live, item 117214617 offered eBayers the opportunity to purchase 200 pounds of uncut cocaine. Bidding in that sale began at $2 million.

While these two sales were noteworthy for the quantity of drugs being offered for sale, a third sale in 2003 was a bit more unusual. A Sacramento, California, man made news after he offered for sale on eBay what he described as poppies to be used for "decorative purposes." A San Francisco forensic scientist begged to differ: "The pods contained opium poppy seeds, which in turn contained morphine." The chemist further indicated that the pods were "shipped ready to be steeped and ingested as a controlled substance with a psychoactive effect." The poppy seller was arrested. Prison sentences in California for such sales can result in up to twenty-five years in jail. There was no mention made of what, if any, charges were brought against the buyer of the opium.

THE CHRISTMAS SPIRIT

It has become tradition in Buckingham Palace for Queen Elizabeth II to give her staff a Christmas pudding. The puddings come from upscale retailer Fortnum & Mason, weigh six and a quarter pounds, and retail for around US$25. Not everyone at the palace qualifies for the gift. The puddings go only to "long-serving staff," and if more recent hires want one they have to purchase their own for retail price.

When one of these puddings, complete with the card signed by Queen Elizabeth and Prince Philip, appeared on eBay UK, the sale apparently did not sit well with the royal family. The auction required an opening bid of £20 but, unfortunately for the seller, came to the attention of palace officials. After a brief investigation it was determined that the individual conducting the sale was a twenty-five-year-old property administrator at the palace who had not worked for the royal family long enough to have earned the privilege of a free pudding. There was also no record of his having purchased one.

According to the *Daily Record*, the investigation determined that the pudding was one of the leftovers that were not given as gifts nor purchased by staff. The worker was summarily fired from his position at the palace for what officials would only call "a breach of security." One wonders what the royal family thought of the auctioning of a slice of wedding cake from Prince Charles and Princess Diana's wedding that took place earlier that month and netted the seller $453 (£258).

CROOKED COP GOES HIGH-TECH

While almost all police officers are honest men and women doing a difficult job the best they can, there have always been a few bad apples amidst their ranks. Hollywood has made hundreds of films portraying crooked cops in cahoots with the criminals they are supposed to arrest. So the fact that an occasional item seized from a suspect ends up in the possession of a police officer would not surprise anyone. It was only a matter of time until a crooked cop turned to eBay to fence his ill-gotten goods.

James Estrella had been a San Diego police officer for more than twelve years when he took a leave of absence to concentrate on what he told fellow officers was his growing Internet business. It seems his Internet business was buying stolen property and then selling it on eBay. Estrella's downfall came as a result of fellow officer Bob Bishop's investigation into the robbery of a church. Doing what was characterized as a routine search on eBay, Bishop found some of the church's stolen property for sale, and the investigation of the seller led to Estrella.

Police in San Diego believe the former officer was selling between eight hundred and a thousand stolen items a month on eBay and bringing in more than $20,000 every thirty days. Ultimately, this high-tech dirty cop earned two years in prison and a $30,000 fine. He also received the second-place award from John

Parson at corporatenarc.com in his top ten ranking of eBay scams. First place was earned by eBay itself for its role in a massive $9.25 million class action lawsuit eBay paid on behalf of its PayPal service's handling of customer complaints.

Get Creative, You Can Sell Anything

To promote and become famous for hosting your own notorious auction, you will need to rely heavily on your powers of creativity. By writing a hilarious description or finding a unique way to photograph your project, you, too, can make a small fortune on eBay and maybe even secure an appearance on national television. Most of the time, fame on eBay is achieved less through the sale of a unique object than by the way in which that object is photographed and described.

The case studies in this section are a smorgasbord of offbeat or common items that, because of their owner's creativity in writing a description, taking a photograph, or simply deciding to sell the item in the first place, became legendary. Do you have a couple of pieces of scrap metal you can weld together to make something that looks like a time machine? Have you ever found a rotting undergarment? Maybe you once discovered an especially long French fry and, instead of washing it down with a soda, stashed the fry away for later.

There is opportunity everywhere you look. From the roll of tape on your office desk to the hole your grandfather dug in the backyard to protect the family in case of nuclear attack—anything and everything, if given the right spin, can make you an eBay legend. Remember, where others see trash, you can find treasure!

A VERY EXPENSIVE BALLPARK FRANK

When the Montreal Expos played their final game in Montreal on September 29, 2004, before moving to Washington, D.C., and renaming themselves the Washington Nationals, fans witnessed a series of final occurrences: the last run scored, the last pitch thrown, the final out made. On that day of "final events" one of the less appreciated last occurrences initially escaped the notice of most of the fans in attendance that day: the last hot dog served at a Montreal Expos baseball game.

Fortunately, one radio station, Energie 102.3, was prepared for this historic opportunity. On the day of the game, the station, located about seventy-five miles from Montreal, gave away four tickets to the final game with the condition that the recipient bring back one of the last hot dogs sold at the ballpark. The fan who scored the tickets lived up to his end of the bargain and the result was auction number 5130853658, titled "LAST DERNIER HOT DOG SOLD VENDU EXPOS MONTREAL."

The auction began on October 13, 2004, and by the time it was over more people had viewed the auction than had attended the team's final three-game home series. Up for sale was the hot dog, "hermetically sealed in a stew of preservatives to ensure it survives forever," a trophy made of the hot dog's original bun, the Styrofoam container the hot dog was sold in, and a mold of the hot dog.

The attention the auction received, which included features on ESPN and all the major Canadian networks, caused the winning bidder, Cirque du Soleil founder Guy Laliberté, to remark, "That hot dog is making more news than the Expos did." That is probably because it is not every day that someone pays $2,605 for a ballpark wiener. The money raised from the auction went to benefit a charity dedicated to buying needy children Christmas presents.

SO THIS IS WHAT THEY MEAN BY DOWNSIZING

In 2000 John D. Freyer, a graduate student from Iowa City, Iowa, became one of eBay's earliest celebrities. It was in

October of that year that Freyer decided to sell virtually everything he owned on eBay. From his furniture to his old records to his used tennis shoes to his half-eaten box of taco shells, almost everything went. Part art project, part social commentary, the sale and his chronicle of what happened to the objects when they left his possession made Freyer famous.

The sale began in October of 2000 when Freyer invited a couple of dozen people to his house for an "Inventory Party." While there, Freyer and his guests rummaged through his belongings and pulled out the items they felt "best represented my life in Iowa City." These items and many more went up for sale on eBay. Freyer then set about chronicling the sales, encouraging his buyers to let him know what became of the items and, sometimes, even visiting his former possessions with their new owners in whatever part of the world they ended up.

Among some of the sale highlights:

- Bidding on all his items started at just $1.
- The highest-priced item sold was a two-volume *Oxford English Dictionary* that went for $183.52.
- Freyer sold almost six hundred items on eBay and another six hundred in a yard sale.
- In total, his sales brought in roughly $6,000.
- At the height of his celebrity, a Web site Freyer set up to help sell his life was receiving over 100,000 visitors a day. During a four-day stretch more than one million people visited the site.

- The University of Iowa's Museum of Art purchased Freyer's two false front teeth for $27 and built a display around them.
- Freyer's stepmother won the auction for Christmas gifts John had purchased for his family but had not yet distributed. She paid $78.

Since the sale ended in August 2001, Freyer has published a book called *All My Life for Sale* that documents his decision to downsize, the items that he sold, the correspondence he has had with his buyers, and his travels to visit his former possessions. As for the half-eaten box of taco shells? They ended up in a cupboard in London, England.

PERFECT GIFT FOR A FAN OF THE WEATHER CHANNEL

When really unusual weather strikes some part of the United States, there are two certainties. First, a devoted group of people from all over the country will ride out the storm on their living room couches watching the Weather Channel. Second, some enterprising soul from the area that was hit will turn to eBay to sell some artifact of the weather.

After Hurricane Frances ran aground north of West Palm Beach, Florida, in September of 2004, those who were unfortunate enough to miss the wrath of the storm were able to pick up a range of items related, in one way or another, to the hurricane. Among the most noteworthy items offered by sellers were a vial of ocean surf collected during the storm, actual rainwater that fell from the sky, the shingle blown off a man's roof by the storm, and the "already dying branches of a native palmetto tree blown down by the unrelenting winds." This seven-inch tree branch apparently was plucked by the seller from the front seat of his car after the tree went through his windshield.

For the discriminating buyer more interested in winter's wrath, opportunities over the years have also been plentiful. In 2001, for instance, after Buffalo was buried under six feet of snow by a string of blizzards, buyers in snow-deprived areas were able to purchase a "pint of official Buffalo snow," although the seller would not guarantee the item's arrival in "unmelted" condition. Further south, when accumulating snow fell for the first time in one hundred years in the Rio Grande Valley of Texas, those who missed out were given the opportunity to purchase a genuine snowball made in the front yard of a man who lived through the monster storm that pummeled the area with three inches of fluffy white powder.

Purchase prices for these weather-related items vary widely from event to event. Perhaps owing to the frequency and amount of snow that typically falls in Buffalo, bidding on the pint of snow offered in 2002 reached just $22.50. The far rarer Texas snow offered in auction 3950669344 drew bids in the millions, although, ultimately, a snowball sold for "only" $92.

FOR THOSE LATE-NIGHT BOMBING RUNS

Apparently when the English Royal Air Force decided its Vulcan nuclear bomber jet airplanes had become a bit outdated, they made some of them available to the public. One of the initial buyers then turned to eBay when he no longer had space for the plane. EBay UK item 5530699633 offered anyone, pilot or no, the opportunity to own his very own Vulcan bomber.

The plane, advertised as "Vulcan bomber XL391 (Complete with engines). Your chance to own a piece of aviation history," came with the caveat that no armaments were included and that no matter how skilled a pilot one might be, the plane did not fly. These two "flaws" apparently did not dampen the enthusiasm of eBayers, and the auction, which took place in November of 2004, attracted hundreds of thousands of viewers.

Vulcans, when they were in service, were operated by a five-man crew, could carry bombs weighing up to 21,000 pounds, and were unique in the early 1960s for their four engines that started simultaneously (thus ensuring that the planes could be airborne quickly in the event of a nuclear attack). The particular plane that was sold had last seen military action during the 1982 Falklands war.

The item had been purchased just after the 1982 conflict by a private citizen who got it directly from the Royal Air Force for £6,000 (US$11,000). It was at that price that the eBay auction began. Bidding was fast and furious, and at one point the asking price rose to over a million pounds. Unfortunately, most of the initial bids were hoaxes and, ultimately, the plane sold for the far more reasonable price of £15,000. The winning bidder was a pub in Dukinfield, Cheshire. The pub planned to display the Vulcan somewhere on its property.

I DON'T KNOW WHAT IT IS BUT I WANT IT

Most people who visit eBay to bid on an item are looking for something in particular or at least something they know they want. This is not true of the people who submitted 150 bids on item 5559938963. Titled simply "Mystery Envelope," the auction went live on February 20, 2005.

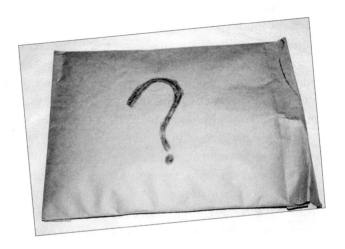

Outside of a plain yellow envelope marked with a question mark, what people were bidding on remains unknown.

The seller said the item was located in Saskatchewan, Canada, but besides that would not divulge anything else about the contents of the envelope, saying, "DON'T email me and ask what is in the envelope, I won't say. DON'T email me after the auction and ask either, I won't say." Remarkably, despite hundreds of questions from eBay members, 115,000 visits, and significant media exposure, the seller offered only one other clue after the price of the auction climbed past $1,000. That clue: that the envelope contained something valuable and was something a lot of people would want.

Despite having no idea of the contents of the envelope, curious eBayers bid the item up to $7,600. The auction's success led to a host of other copycat auctions. Some items were guaranteed to be worth a certain amount of money, and some substituted a safe or a chest or a drawer for the envelope, but none generated the same level of publicity as the original.

Today this one-of-a-kind envelope and its contents reside with the auction's winner, GoldenPalace.com. Representatives of the online casino say only, "Time will tell if they choose to disclose the contents of this mysterious package to the world."

ALL THE TIME IN THE WORLD

Time travel has always been a dream of mankind. In March of 2005, that dream seemed a lot closer to being reality thanks to one eBay seller. Titled "TIME MACHINE! For Time travel? very low reserve," item 5563490518 captured the imagination of eBayers all over the world.

According to the seller, he was offering what he believed to be a time machine invented in the year 2239 by one Dr. J. S. Strauss. Unfortunately, the time machine appeared to have caught fire or was otherwise damaged and was in nonworking condition. The seller also believed that this unfortunate event had trapped Dr. Strauss in the early part of the twentieth century where, based on pictures found with the machine, he had taken up residence.

The seller said he discovered the machine when, while remodeling his bathroom, he pulled the contraption from beneath his floor. The seller was able to identify the damaged contraption as a time machine based on a helpful brass plaque conveniently attached to the machine, providing the purpose of the machine, the name of the inventor, and the year in which it was invented.

During the weeklong sale, more than 375,000 people visited the auction. Some believed the item to be genuine while others were naturally skeptical. In response to a question from one eBayer asking, "I can't decide whether you are a comedy genius, entrepreneur, conman, or just a complete twat. Which is it?" the seller answered, "I'm just an average guy who just happens to have found a time machine under his house." Perhaps because it was broken, the time machine sold for what seems to be the very reasonable price of $647.59.

MAYBE THIS IS VICTORIA'S SECRET

When you remodel a home, you do not generally expect to have mangled and rotting undergarments fall from the ceiling. But when they do, you should know that there is always a home for them on eBay.

As the purveyor of auction number 2948761136 in September 2003 described it at the time of her discovery, she was in the process of pulling down the last of some tiles in her dining room's ceiling, which needed to be replaced because of water damage. When the final tile was removed, a pile of, as she put it, "ceiling flotsam" poured out. Among the contents of this outpouring was "this rotted, nasty, completely disgusting female garment." Her auction names the product "Weird Gross Bra That Fell from My Ceiling."

After assuring potential bidders that she had lived in the home for more than fifteen years and had "never once stored my dainties under the floorboards," she went on to write such a comical description of possible reasons that someone might want this item that more than 120,000 people stopped by her auction to view this one-of-a-kind piece of lingerie.

EBay initially pulled the item because, according to the company, the description had a "fetish" element to it, but the company allowed the auction to be reposted after this "element" was removed. The bra ended up fetching more than a hundred dollars but its whereabouts today are unknown.

WHAT DO YOU WANT ON YOUR TOMBSTONE?

It may sound like a morbid question, but it is exactly the one Disneyland posed to potential bidders on eBay item 2277241669. The auction, titled "DISNEYLAND Haunted Mansion 1000th Ghost Experience," put up for grabs the right to personalize a tombstone in the Haunted Mansion attraction at Disneyland. According to the item's description, "For the first time ever, a lucky member of the public will win the opportunity to become a permanent part of a classic Disneyland attraction!"

The tombstone would bear the owner's first name and an epithet agreed upon with the creative design team in charge of the exhibit. In addition to becoming the thousandth ghost in the attraction, the winner and a guest would also be given a trip to the Magic Kingdom for the graveside ceremony and invited to be the "ghost of honor" at the annual Haunted Mansion Holiday.

Bidding kicked off on October 14, 2004, with an offer of $750 made by none other than famed horror author Clive Barker. Unfortunately for Barker, his first bid was nowhere near sufficient to win the one-of-a-kind memorial. By the time the auction ended a week later, more than 60,000 people had visited the sale and bidding ended at $37,400. The successful suitor was Cary "Jay" Sharp, a doctor and health-care attorney from Baton Rouge, Louisiana. His tombstone now reads, JAY. DOCTOR-LAWYER LEGAL CLERK. FOREVER BURIED IN HIS WORK. All money raised by the auction went to benefit the Boys and Girls Clubs of America.

TAPE BALL

Have you ever dreamed of owning the world's largest ball of tape? If so, then item 5572335347 may be just what you have been searching for. Put up for sale on April 9, 2005, the giant tape ball was billed as a possible world record breaker and required an opening bid of just 1 cent. That plus the $150 it was estimated shipping the item would cost.

According to the seller's description, the ball was made up of one thousand rolls of tape, weighed in at sixty pounds, and, while "Guinness lists the largest tape ball as 80 pounds, that ball is made out of masking tape, which is like 4 times the size of the tape we use." The item came complete with an application for the Guinness World Records and five hundred rolls of unused tape. It also came with the Web site www.balloftape.com, which documented the item's creation.

When asked how long it took to create the giant tape ball, the seller answered that about fifteen people had worked on the ball and it had taken about five years to get the ball to its current girth. Thirty-five thousand people logged in to the auction and the ball of tape received 26 bids. Ultimately the monster ball was purchased for $1,025. That's a far cry from the penny bid that started the auction, but keep in mind that a roll of tape costs between a dollar and a dollar fifty, which means the one thousand rolls it took to create the Goliath of tape balls and the five hundred unused rolls cost more than the final sale price, and that does not include the countless hours of labor necessary to complete such a historic project.

THE WORLD'S MOST EXPENSIVE PAIR OF JEANS

Levi's has been making and selling jeans since 1873. In 2001 the company became the consumer and paid what is believed to be a record amount for a single pair of jeans. Of course, this was not just any old pair of jeans. It was believed to be the oldest pair of jeans in existence. The antique article of apparel had been found buried in the mud in a Nevada mining town and was made of nine-ounce denim at the Amoskeag Mill yard in Manchester, New Hampshire, between 1880 and 1885.

The auction for the jeans, sponsored by the History Channel, began May 17, 2001, and ran for seven days. Potential bidders had to register to be eligible to participate in the bidding.

Despite a fifteen-inch gash in the crotch area and two holes in the knee, pre-auction estimates priced the pair of pants at between $25 and $35,000. Perhaps due to the significant media coverage the auction attracted and the emphasis placed on it by the History Channel, as the auction came to a close a bidding war erupted between several last-minute contenders and the price of the jeans skyrocketed to $46,532. Although it is unlikely we will see this particular pair of jeans modeled anytime soon, after the auction this piece of American and fashion history went on display at Levi's flagship office in San Francisco.

FOR THE JET-SETTING CROWD

It weighs 62,000 pounds, travels at five hundred miles an hour, and can fly more than 3,500 miles without refueling. First built in 1967 by the Grumman Corporation, the Gulfstream II became an instant success despite its initial price tag of $2 million (roughly $11.5 million in today's currency). This jet also holds another distinction: in 2001, one of these planes recorded the highest confirmed selling price ever on eBay, $4.9 million.

Tyler Jet, a small company in Texas, was the seller of the used twelve-seat version of the Gulfstream II. After 97 bids the plane was purchased by a group operating charter flights out of Africa. The final sale price eclipsed by more than three times the previous record held by a 1909 Honus Wagner baseball card sold in 2000 for $1.265 million. The price commanded by the Honus Wagner collectible remains the most ever paid for a baseball card.

Among other eBay items notable for their high price tags and verifiable sales was the October 2004 auction of a rare Ferrari Enzo, one of only 399 ever made. The sports car had just 400 kilometers on its odometer. Sold on Swiss eBay, it recorded the highest price ever paid for an item on an eBay Europe site: $950,000. In the United Kingdom, the single item that attracted the highest purchase price was an empty handbag formerly owned by Margaret Thatcher, purchased by the lucky winner for $185,000. Money from that sale went to support Breast Cancer Care and Research Fund.

THE WORLD'S LONGEST FRENCH FRY?

Long before McDonald's decided to auction off a French fry that looked like Abraham Lincoln on Yahoo's auction site, there was eBay item number 2937200633. The seller did not claim that he was certain that the item advertised as the "World's Longest French Fry" actually was the longest French fry, but he did say it was currently registered with Guinness World Records "as a possible record breaker."

This majestic piece of fried potato was rumored to be nearly seven inches long and said by the auction purveyor to hail from a Wisconsin fast-food outlet. The establishment was later identified by the *Wausau Daily Herald* as Culver's restaurant located in Wisconsin Rapids.

The famous French fry was the talk of Internet chat rooms in the early summer of 2003, and thousands of people tuned in to eBay to view the freakish specimen, which was featured in news reports around the globe. The auction ended with a $202.50 winning bid.

Since the auction there have been a host of challengers. One of the most serious contenders has been an upstart from the same restaurant that gave birth to the original colossal French fry. The second French fry, rumored to be eight inches in length, was sold for $250 during a daylong radio station auction in February of 2005 by WQBF 97.3 FM. Money from this second auction went to support a local food pantry.

IF YOU WON THE AUCTION YOU ALREADY KNOW WHAT THIS CHAPTER IS ABOUT

Think of the power you would wield if you had the ability to know the unspoken thoughts of others. Thanks to the seller of item 5578647786, titled "MIND READING MACHINE? for minds?" one lucky eBayer was given this opportunity.

According to the item description, the mind-reading machine was discovered wrapped in an old bedsheet in the seller's attic. Apparently it was invented in the year 2282 and brought back to our era in a time-traveling mishap. (This gizmo was reportedly invented by the same genius who created the time machine we have already read about

in this book.) Unfortunately for the man who found the machine, he could not figure out how to make the device work, hence the sale.

As the seller said, "This electronic stuff from the future is hard for us to understand, so that's why I am selling the mind-reading machine." The seller was able to tell that the item actually was a mind-reading machine thanks to the handy-dandy plaque found in the vicinity of the item stating when it was invented and by whom.

Apparently the device weighed roughly six pounds and was made of copper, metal, and plastic. EBay pulled the item for a brief time because the title of the auction in its first iteration contained the phrase "like time machine," which violated the company's policy against search manipulation. As the seller explained in his apology for the auction's delisting, using that phrase in the item description would basically means that anybody searching for a time machine would have found this item, which is clearly not a time machine, hence its removal.

More than 22,000 people visited the second iteration of the auction, which closed on May 13, 2005. The new owner paid $710 and is actively searching for someone who can make the device work.

THE STRING CHEESE INCIDENT

Normally lawyers ask prospective clients for a retainer in advance of agreeing to represent a case in a court of law. On June 17, 2002, an innovative eBayer attempted to reverse this traditional arrangement.

According to the seller of item number 174223570, titled "Represent Tainted Borden Elsie String Cheese," prospective buyers were bidding on the opportunity to act as the seller's lawyer in what he or she must have felt was a can't-lose case. Apparently the individual seeking the legal representation had purchased a package of Borden String Cheese and then "noticed what appears to be a hair from a human (head cheese?) bovine or rodent." This hair was supposedly completely embedded in the cheese when the package was opened. The minimum opening bid necessary to obtain the privilege to take on the case was $500.

As the author of this auction made quite clear, the winning bidder would not be getting the cheese—only the opportunity to represent him or her in what seemed to be an inevitable court date. Needless to say, the seller required the winning bidder to be a licensed attorney, although he did not specify what state the attorney needed to be licensed in.

The seller also reserved the right to disqualify the winner if his or her qualifications were not up to the task of recouping significant monetary compensation for the psychological scarring the incident had apparently wreaked on the original buyer of the befouled product.

Unfortunately for the seller, according to *USA Today*, he found no takers as "eBay authorities removed the auction because of the frivolous attention it drew." Surprisingly enough, for an auction that attracted so much attention there were no bids, real or otherwise. Perhaps those who have a tendency to bid up notorious items such as this one were intimidated by the apparently litigious propensities of the seller. There is no word on whether or not there was a settlement of the grievance regarding the hair in the string cheese.

Dealing in Real Estate

Over the past five years, the United States has experienced what can only be described as a real estate boom. Housing and land values have skyrocketed and, as one would expect, entrepreneurial eBayers have been at the cutting edge of real estate transactions.

Every day thousands of real estate offerings, from million-dollar mansions to small log cabins without electricity or running water, go up for sale on eBay. You can buy a beach home in the

Caribbean, a winter chalet in the Alps, or a time share in the South Pacific, all without ever having been within ten thousand miles of the property.

There are thousands of listings each day, but once in a while a property goes up for sale that is so unique it attracts worldwide media attention. If you have a home once owned by a celebrity, eBay is the place to advertise it. Sometimes it may not be an individual home but a whole town that goes up for sale. If you can get your hands on your very own village, it might be your ticket to fame.

If those two options are not possible, you might want to consider auctioning off something you don't own. EBayers have been making news selling such things as states and countries for years now. EBay will certainly remove the listing, but the humor value may garner you the attention needed to create a world-famous sale.

One suggestion, though: if you are serious about actually selling your property, make sure you limit bidding to preapproved buyers. Real estate sales, especially when they revolve around property once owned by a celebrity, seem to attract potential buyers whose eyes are far bigger than their checkbooks.

A HOUSE

On any given day the collector of Bob Dylan merchandise can sign on to eBay and find a large selection of Dylan-autographed memorabilia—posters, photos, and other items in one way or another associated with the rock icon. But on May 24, 2001, Dylan's sixtieth birthday, the discriminating Dylan fan was given the opportunity to purchase something advertised as "a must-have for the die-hard Dylan fan": the singer's childhood home, a.k.a. item number 1600991971.

The home, located in Duluth, Minnesota, was put up for sale by Kathy Burns, who had originally planned to live in it or turn it into a museum. Among the 1,800-square-foot duplex's features were views of Lake Superior, excellent interior woodcraft, and even Bob Dylan's initials, said to have been carved into the wall by the singer himself when he was a child.

After an opening bid of $85,000, the house sold for $94,600, giving Burns, who had purchased the collectible dwelling for $62,000 in 1996, a nice profit. This sale also seems to have started a trend. Among other notables whose former homes have since been offered on eBay are those of Jimi Hendrix, Nirvana's Kurt Cobain, Johnny Carson, Madonna, Eminem, Brett Favre, Susan B. Anthony, and even the homes of the three most recent presidents, Bill Clinton, George W. Bush, and George H. Bush. It should be noted that only one home belonging to the Bushes went on the market. It just happens that both presidents at one point lived there.

A TOWN

A few days before Christmas in 2002, a town few people outside of far northern California had ever heard of suddenly became international news. The reason? Someone was selling it on eBay. Really. Founded in 1871, Bridgeville, California, had been privately owned for nearly a century, and when Joe and Elizabeth Lapple, the owners of the town since 1972, could not sell it via conventional methods, they turned to the online auction site.

Located amid towering redwoods, Bridgeville is in rural Humboldt County, California, about 250 miles north of San Francisco. When the logging industry crumbled, few people remained behind and the town began to die. The post office was the only business still in operation.

The town consisted of eighty-two acres, a mile and a half of riverbank, more than a dozen houses and cabins, and a post office. Bidding started at $5,000, and by the time the auction closed after a month, the sale had garnered more than 250 bids and generated a final sale price of $1,777,877.

Bridgeville may have been the first town to be sold on eBay, but it was not the last. Since the auction concluded, more than a dozen towns, located mostly in western states, have changed hands through eBay. Unfortunately, the sellers of these towns have had mixed success in seeing the sales through to closure.

In the case of Bridgeville, the Lapples and their real estate broker could not contact the winning bidder and, after reaching out to other contenders without success, put the property back on the market a year later, but not on eBay, for just $850,000. When asked why they did not relist on eBay, particularly since the auction had generated so much interest and the town had nearly sold for double the current asking price, the Lapples' legal representative stated, "You have no idea who [the buyers] are, if they're real or they're bogus."

A STATE

Who wouldn't want to own his or her own state? Auction 2372779353, titled "Entire State of West Virginia," went on the block January 12, 2004, and within two days had attracted 56 bids, bumping the cost from an initial asking price of $1 to nearly $100 million. Within minutes of the release of the AP's story on the auction, eBay officials got wind of the prank and pulled the sale, saying the seller could not possibly possess the state.

The seller, known only as fishstuffnthings, claimed that as emperor of West Virginia he had been appointed steward of the sale and that those who chose to participate in the auction would not be able to acquire governing rights or "have the ability to change the state flag, bird, or so on." The purchaser would, however, have bragging rights, since he was willing to relinquish to the auction's winner his title of emperor.

The auction even caught the attention of West Virginia governor Bob Wise. The spokesperson for the governor, Amy Shuler Goodwin, commented, according to the AP, "As an eBay consumer myself . . . that's a heck of a bargain." Unfortunately for the high bidder, $100 million would just be the beginning of his or her investment. West Virginia was forecasting a $120 million deficit for 2005.

A FORT

With the Cold War over, many communities around the world were forced to ask themselves, "What do we do with those pesky underground nuclear bunkers?" The answer for several communities in the United Kingdom? Sell them on eBay.

In all, thirteen former nuclear bunkers were put up for sale on eBay's UK site in the spring of 2003. The bunkers were originally designed to hold three-man volunteer teams from the Royal Observer Corps who were charged with detecting nuclear detonations and monitoring radioactive fallout. The enclosures have no gas, electricity, or running water, but they do come with a chemical toilet and are located fifteen feet underground. The bunkers measure approximately 7½ feet by 15 feet, thus providing about 110 square feet of living space.

The auctions of the bunkers attracted hundreds of bids from people around the world who had all sorts of possible uses planned for them—for instance, a vacation home or a place for students seeking cheap living space. Final prices were not so cheap. One bunker located in Cumbria County in northwest England sold for £25,100 (roughly US$45,000). The more frugal minded would be happy to learn that a bunker in Stannington, Northumberland, was had for only £5,600 (US$10,000).

The ways in which the current owners of these bunkers are using them varies dramatically, but should you desire to visit one of these Cold War relics at least one accommodates overnight visitors. The price for up to three guests is £160 (US$290) a night.

A BASE

It cost tens of millions of dollars to build in the 1960s, but for a limited time on eBay a cost-conscious eBay shopper had the opportunity to walk away with a complete twenty-six-acre Atlas E military complex, located near the town of Wamego, Kansas, for a fraction of the original cost. According to the description of item 4301229032, Atlas E bases are the most desirable of all decommissioned nuclear silos, which through army fire sales have made their way into private hands.

The Kansas site features more than 15,000 square feet of underground space spread across two locations connected by a hundred-foot tunnel. In addition to the subterranean space, above ground are two 4,000-square-foot warehouses, a roughly half-mile-long paved road, and a grass landing strip for planes.

The site was designed to withstand a nuclear blast fifty times stronger than the one dropped on Hiroshima. Other features include a 5,400-square-foot command center complete with escape hatches, concrete walls that range in thickness from eighteen inches to six feet, and a missile bay with twenty-foot ceilings. As an added bonus, the ceilings are retractable owing to the fact that, should it ever have been necessary to launch nuclear missiles from the site, there needed to be a way to breach the surface.

Apparently the military complex also comes with quite a history. According to newspaper articles that surfaced in response to the auction, this site was on the brink of becoming one of the nation's largest LSD factories before a drug bust went down in 2000. One DEA spokesperson was quoted as saying that the owner of the site had put nearly $2 million into the complex, and among the many improvements made was the installation of "an LSD lab inside which could have produced one-third of the world's LSD supply."

Buyer beware, as the criminal history was not mentioned in the eBay description. However, it may have had something to do with the fact that, despite a final closing price of $1.5 million, the base remained advertised well after the auction closed, so the sale probably did not go through.

A GENTLEMEN'S CLUB

In 2000 a gentlemen's club called Climax, located in rural Pennsylvania about forty-five miles east of Pittsburgh, became the first and only establishment of its kind to offer a "drive-thru service." Patrons simply pulled up to the window and the exotic dancer performed while the audience remained in the car. This service gained the establishment significant media attention and led to, among other things, a feature article in *Time* magazine entitled "Hold the Pickles, Please," mentions on the Jay Leno, David Letterman, and Howard Stern shows, and even a question in the twentieth anniversary edition of Trivial Pursuit.

In 2005 the strip club went on the market. The only logical place for this sale to occur? EBay, of course. Item 4353224520 was titled "Climax World Famous Gentlemen's Club and NUDE Drive Thru" and went live on January 25. Included in the sale were the license to conduct all nude club performances, the 2,000-square-foot building, and approximately 1.1 acres of land. Financial records for the business were not made available.

Bidding began at $299,000, although there was a reserve. Over the month-long sale, the auction was the most heavily viewed on the eBay system; more than 180,000 potential bidders checked out the sale, which was promoted at www.climaxredtop.com. Despite 52 bids and a final offer of $501,900, the item failed to meet the reserve set by the owner and did not sell. For the record, no pictures of the dancers were featured on eBay.

Benefit from Technology

Keeping up to date on the current trends in technology is essential for businesses of all types in today's modern economy. The same holds true for those seeking fame and fortune on eBay. As the case studies in this lesson demonstrate, modern technology and the debates that arise surrounding it have spawned some of the most notorious eBay auctions.

Have you had a spat with a major technology company? Using eBay might be a way to extract some measure of justice. Do you want a cheap way to promote the very latest in technology and raise capital in the process? A carefully constructed sales pitch might land you and your company in newspapers around the world.

Since eBay is a survivor of the dot-com era, it is no surprise that technology-related products sell well on eBay. Whenever the latest and greatest piece of technology is released, it is certain that even if nobody else can keep it in stock, you will have a chance to purchase it on eBay. For the seller of such items, not only are large payoffs possible, but there is also the possibility of presiding over your very own auction-driven media frenzy.

8 6 7 - 5 3 0 9

The phone number was made famous by a 1981 song written by one-hit wonder Tommy Tutone. The chorus, "Jenny, I got your number, I need to make you mine. Jenny, don't change your number, 867-5309 (867-5309) 867-5309 (867-5309)," was something listeners could not get out of their heads. When a cell-phone user was able to procure the number (in New York City, area code 212), he got the bright idea that someone might pay good money for it. The only logical place to find out what the famous phone digits were worth? EBay, where else.

Item number 3077991790 went live in January of 2004. For the right price, the description said, the winning bidder would "get the greatest number in the greatest city."

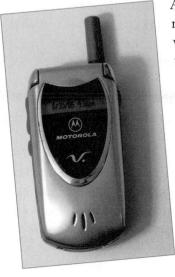

According to the seller, the new owner of this number would probably have to deal with several phone calls a week from people asking for Jenny, but apparently a number of bidders thought that sort of inconvenience was well worth the price of owning the famous seven digits. After the auction was featured on *Good Morning America*, half a million people tuned in to the auction, bidding reached more than $200,000, and owners of the number in several other area codes also tried to get in on the act by putting their numbers up for sale on eBay.

Unfortunately, after five days eBay was forced to pull the auctions because of legal questions surrounding the ownership of phone numbers. According to a Verizon spokesperson, the company, not the user, owns the phone number and therefore the resale of 867-5309 would not be permitted.

TO THE MOON, ALICE! TO THE MOON!

Neil Armstrong's footprint, the American flag, and now your garbage! Item 3810433079 was offered in April 2004 by a Nevada-based company called Orbital Development. Through its Moon Crash Project, the company was offering the high bidder the opportunity to crash twenty pounds of his or her own personal cargo on the moon.

According to the firm's Web site, the project would "use a Russian aerospace contractor's commercial test launch vehicle" to transport the material on a direct flight from the earth to the near side of the moon. The flight would take four to six days and during this time the ship would beam back photos every four to six minutes. The impact time would be scheduled to coincide with either sunrise or sunset to ensure "superior photography."

According to Leonard David, writing for Space.com, the president of Orbital Development believed that "the Moon Crash Project would probably be attractive to some bored rich guy who is tired of playing with his radio-controlled model airplanes and wants to move up to the next level."

Bidding began at $6.2 million and ran for ten days. Despite the media attention, the item did not sell. Nonetheless, Orbital still welcomes inquiries from people interested in arranging a launch. One cautionary note for potential buyers: although Orbital says it will make every effort to ensure that the buyer's package remains intact upon impact, there are no guarantees the material will not

be destroyed when the rocket explodes on the moon's surface.

IT'S A BIRD, IT'S A PLANE, IT'S . . . IT'S . . . YOUR OWN PERSONAL STRAP-ON AIRCRAFT?

Trek Aerospace is a small California company seeking to de-
velop "Personal Air Vehicles" for civilian and military use.
One of the outfit's early prototypes weighed three hundred
pounds, could hover for more than two hours, and could
travel at speeds of up to sixty-nine miles an hour.
According to CNN, "The company's dream is to one day
have a sky buzzing with SoloTrek flyers. Future versions
of the machines could transport soldiers over land mines
or help commuters avoid rush-hour traffic." Well before
this dream would become a reality, eBayers were given the
chance to own their very own prototype of the futuristic
vehicle.

Item 2153209735 went live January 10, 2003, and the
sale immediately caught the attention of the news media
and general public, who were fascinated by the mecha-
nism, which seemed to many to be straight out of a science
fiction movie. Interest in the auction was tremendous. The
opening bid was $50,000 and within forty-eight hours of
going live the bidded price had climbed to more than $1
million. This despite the fact that the device had been dis-
abled and the sellers required the potential purchaser to
promise not to try to use the machine. According to Trek

Aerospace, it was simply too early in the development process to begin unauthorized flights, and any attempt to use the machine would be extremely hazardous.

The company had put the device up for sale in an effort to raise much-needed cash for future research and development. Unfortunately for the sellers, interest in the auction was so intense that bidding was manipulated by hoaxers. Although the price at one point climbed beyond $6 million, it was impossible to authenticate the bids. Ultimately the auction ended in controversy. The aftermath brought significant attention to the issue of how best to deal with fraudulent/hoax bidders in high-profile sales such as this one.

TAKING ON GOLIATH

Mike Rowe was a seventeen-year-old high school senior from Canada who ran a Web site at MikeRowesoft.com. He thought the moniker was a clever play on his name. When Microsoft got wind of the site, the company thought that the phonetic domain name infringed on its copyright and demanded that Mike Rowe hand the name over to them and offered to pay the $10 it cost Mike to register the domain. Mike countered with a request for $10,000, which gave Microsoft the legal ammunition to argue that Mike had purposefully registered the domain name with the express intent of profiting from it. The computer giant threatened to take the teenager to court and sent a twenty-five-page legal brief to Mike detailing its case against him. Mike Rowe went to the press and the disagreement became a lot of bad publicity for Microsoft, but, eventually, the two sides came to an agreement and the teen settled for an X-Box, free Microsoft certification training, and reimbursement for the cost of setting up a new site.

And that was the end of that. Or so everyone thought until a couple of days later when Mike Rowe, his fifteen minutes of fame apparently not yet over, turned up in the news again. This time he made headlines for the auction he was running on eBay. For sale: item number 3382073018, a book full of documents related to his conflict with Microsoft. Among the papers were the emails he had received from Microsoft, his responses, and, most notably, the twenty-five-page legal brief sent by Microsoft lawyers detailing the company's case against him.

The auction was viewed by hundreds of thousands of people worldwide and bidding went to well over $20 million before Mike put some checks in place to separate the legitimate bids from the hoaxes. Ultimately many of the bidders could not be traced and Mike sold the documents for a "mere" $1,037.

MONITORING EMPLOYEE MORALE

In 1999 it was a dot-com world, and what better place than eBay could there be for a team of technology experts to glean the most value for their services? An apparently serious group of Bay Area techies decided they were ready to leave their current positions en masse, and the best way to command the highest possible salaries was to sell their services to the highest bidder.

The auction caught the attention of major newspapers, magazines, and television shows around the country and, according to *Time* magazine, even helped convince the Monster.com founder to implement a "talent service" where contractors and freelancers could auction themselves off to the highest bidder.

The techies' auction description read in part: "Team of 16 employees from major ISP willing to leave as a group," and it kicked off with an asking price of $3.14 million. That price included the salaries of a director as well as a set of engineers and administrators. The winning bidder would also have to pony up a $320,000 signing bonus and offer a competitive 401K. The team was apparently unwilling to relocate, specifying that their new positions had to be in Silicon Valley or the San Francisco Bay Area.

The sale never went through because the sellers pulled their auction before it could end. Nevertheless, the fact that it was offered at all during this era of "irrational exuberance" had columnists and television commentators from coast to coast discussing the new wave of employee-employer relations. After all, according to *Time* magazine, "Sure, athletes are bought and sold all the time; but it sounds ridiculous to shop for a UNIX programmer or architect. Yet the timing is perfect for such a bold experiment in the burgeoning field of e-cruiting."

This bold new world has yet to come to pass, but at least the group of job seekers had the foresight to market their wares on one of the dot-com boom's few success stories. There is no word on what work conditions were like at the sellers' place of employment to have caused sixteen of them to form a pact to quit in unison.

EBAY FOR SALE

In 1999 eBay was already a successful company. It was one of the few profitable Internet-based firms, had earned a respectable $10.8 million the year before on sales of $225 million, and had an irrational market cap of around $20 billion, due, in large part, to dot-com fever. The auction site itself, however, was still in its innocent stage. Many of the controls eBay now has in place to regulate its online marketplace had not yet been created.

So it was that auction number 168272199 came to be. Up for sale: eBay itself. In a time when eBay was coming under increased scrutiny for a number of illegal and fraudulent auctions that had recently been consummated through its site, someone using the seller name Misone put the company up for sale. Remarkably, the auction did not come to the attention of eBay management, or the media, until the auction had run its course and bidding was closed. Seven bids were placed and one lucky winner acquired the multibillion-dollar company for a mere $1.25.

According to Greg Sandoval writing for CNET news,

when informed of the sale eBay spokesperson Kevin Pursgolve deadpanned, "We're worth every cent," before further commenting that the auction obviously went against eBay policy prohibiting the sale of items one does not actually own. This is one case, among a whole host of ill-faring dot-com-boom-and-bust stories, where the company is still worth more than the auction's $1.25 sale price.

LESSON X

Know Your Buyer

To maximize your success as a seller you need to understand what makes potential buyers tick. What is it about one auction that makes someone bid while a second auction of the same exact item results in an unsold listing?

Some eBayers are able to achieve fame not through the sale of a notorious item, but by making their buying habits legendary. Are you willing to serve jail time for stalking the winner of an item you covet for your own? Do you have access to someone else's eBay account and credit card, and would you fancy top-shelf items such as a helicopter? Do you have thousands of dollars to spend on outrageous items, thus buying publicity for yourself through the news stories generated by such auctions?

Whether you seek to appeal to the buyers whose stories appear on the following pages or wish to become like the select group of sellers highlighted in this lesson's case studies, the successful creation of a notorious auction requires that you keep in mind that there are always two people involved in every eBay auction. Remember, though, when posting notorious eBay items, seller beware, you never know who is lurking behind those eBay monikers!

A ONE-OF-A-KIND PROMOTION

While the grilled cheese Madonna and the pope's former car were making headlines around the world, one buyer was becoming nearly as notorious as the items it has purchased. GoldenPalace.com has outbid the competition in dozens of the most famous of eBay auctions, including a number of those featured within the pages of this book. Through the widespread attention these purchases attracted, the casino has made itself and its business a household name.

In addition to promoting its business, GoldenPalace.com also uses the auctions to support charitable causes. By either purchasing items when the proceeds go to charity or through hosting innovative charitable fund-raisers that somehow revolve around an item purchased via eBay, the company has raised millions of dollars for worthwhile causes worldwide.

GoldenPalace.com also gives many of the more famous auctions extended life after their time on eBay ends. A section of the casino's Web site is set up for the eBay devotee. A visitor can take a tour of the company's online museum dedicated to past purchases, read stories about how the items are currently being used, and even reminisce by reviewing actual screen captures cached by the company that show the auctions during their heyday.

GoldenPalace.com's promotional campaign has become so well known among members of the eBay community that the company reports it receives hundreds of notifications weekly from sellers of eBay oddities hoping to attract the company's attention. The campaign has been featured in Keith Olbermann's countdown on MSNBC that looked at cutting-edge advertising strategies, and is beginning to appear as a case study in successful promotional campaigns at some of the nation's top business schools.

What, one might wonder, does GoldenPalace.com's primary business—gambling—have to do with eBay? Maybe not a whole lot, but if you ask the person who sold the grilled cheese Madonna for $28,000 or the man who sold the pope's former car for more than $200,000, these two sellers would both probably say they hit the jackpot on eBay.

HOW DEREK JETER'S NAME CAME TO BE AN OBSCENITY

It seemed like a good idea at the time. When Fleet Bank terminated the contract giving it naming rights to the arena where both the Boston Celtics and the Boston Bruins play their home games, the owners of the former Boston Garden arena decided to auction off daily naming rights on eBay. All proceeds were to go to charity. Everything was running smoothly until New York attorney Kerry Konrad won the right to name the building on March 1, 2005, with a high bid of $2,325.

An ardent Yankees fan, Konrad apparently saw his win as an opportunity to fan the flames of a twenty-five-year rivalry with former college classmates who are Boston Red Sox fans, because he announced to his friends and the world that he planned to name the arena in honor of New York Yankees shortstop Derek Jeter. Given the bitter rivalry between baseball fans in Boston and New York, the prospect of naming anything in Boston after an arch nemesis did indeed cause quite a commotion.

Caught in a bind between honoring a "legally binding" auction and causing outrage and possible rioting in Boston, the executives in charge of the Boston arena found a unique out. According to Darren Rovel of ESPN, Richard A. Krezwick, president and chief executive of the Fleet Center, said, "We decided that all the names had to be G rated, and this name was determined to be obscene and vulgar."

With Derek Jeter off the table, one of Konrad's former roommates, this one a Red Sox fan, stepped forward and put an additional $6,275 on top of Konrad's bid and, on March 1, 2005, named the arena the Jimmy Fund Center. All proceeds raised went to the Jimmy Fund, which "supports the fight against cancer in children and adults at Boston's Dana-Farber Cancer Institute."

For those keeping track, the total amount raised was $8,600, an amount intended to memorialize Boston's eighty-six-year-old "Curse of the Bambino," which was broken in 2004 when the Red Sox won their first World Series since selling Babe Ruth to the Yankees.

THIS PROBABLY WON'T HELP THE CREDIT RATING

Despite all of the preemptive steps eBay takes to keep false bidders and ID impersonators from the auction action, occasionally someone slips through the cracks. Perhaps the most famous eBay pretender was a thirteen-year-old boy who gained national notoriety in the spring of 2002.

As his school year at Beaver Middle School in eastern Ohio was coming to an end, the bored student found an innovative way to use his school computer: he went on a shopping spree on eBay. While such occurrences are probably common, the student came to the attention of authorities because of the amount of money he spent: almost $2 million.

Using a password given to him by a friend, the young

man hacked into the friend's mother's eBay account and immediately began racking up bills. Among other things, his purchases included a $1.1 million helicopter, a $199,000 jet, a pickup truck, and multiple motorcycles. Authorities were alerted to the scam when the owner of the helicopter called the true eBay account holder and asked her how she would like to pay for the purchase. It remains unclear how the boy, lacking any sort of pilot or driver's license, intended to use his acquisitions.

SORE LOSER

There was seemingly nothing out of the ordinary when on June 23, 2002, a collection of nearly five hundred matching used band and dance uniforms sold to a New York buyer for $360. But as the events that ensued show, when you are trying to win an auction, you never really know who or what your competition is.

Apparently a New Orleans man who had hoped to purchase the collection could not come to grips with the fact that the outfits had slipped through his grasp. After several months of trying, unsuccessfully, to convince the winner to part with his treasure through such persuasive tactics as calling the winner a cross-dressing homo, the sore loser traveled more than 1,300 miles to confront his rival in person.

According to a Poughkeepsie, New York, prosecutor, the would-be buyer broke into the winner's apartment on July 3, 2003, and when he found his nemesis was not home, threatened the winner's wife with a gun. The man left without incident by taxi and was picked up by detectives a short time later. For his part, the bidder-turned-burglar claimed the gun had fallen from his pants accidentally while he was reaching for a piece of paper. Days before he was scheduled to go to trial on charges of burglary, criminal possession of a weapon, and coercion, facing a minimum prison term of five to twenty-five years, the foiled bidder pleaded guilty in exchange for a promise that he would go to jail for no more than one to three years.

HOW A BROKEN LASER POINTER CHANGED THE WORLD

EBay has changed the way people shop and has proven that no matter how strange or useless an item might seem, there is almost always someone out there who will see treasure where everyone else sees junk. A case in point: one of the first items ever sold on eBay was a broken laser pointer.

This item was put up for sale by eBay founder Pierre Omidyar in 1995 on the site that was then called AuctionWeb. According to eBay legend, Omidyar had bought the laser pointer to play with his pet cat. Using the device he traced red lines over the carpet and up the walls of his home while his cat tried futilely to capture the laser. After two weeks the $30 laser pointer quit working and Pierre was left with a useless electronic device.

But Pierre did not do what most anyone else would

have done—check the device to find out if its warranty had expired and then throw it away. Instead he put it up for auction on the Internet. After fourteen days the device sold for $14. Pleased but mystified as to why someone would want a broken laser pointer, Pierre emailed the buyer to first ensure he knew that the item did not work, and, if he did, to find out what had inspired the purchase. According to Pierre, "He said he liked playing around with things, fixing them." It was then that Omidyar knew he was on to something.

From this auspicious beginning, billions of items have followed the laser pointer to auction and eBay has become perhaps the world's most successful Internet business. As for the laser pointer, its whereabouts today are unknown, but if the anonymous buyer of the device should ever decide to put it up for sale on eBay, the significance of the item as a collectible could fetch a very hefty profit.

Closing the Deal

Congratulations! Your studies are complete and you are
now ready to go out and create your very
own notorious eBay auction. As you begin
your search for that special item that will bring
you fame and fortune, remember to always keep
an eye on eBay's legions of sellers. New items appear every day, and over the coming months and
years there is little doubt that many, many more
eBay sales, sellers, and buyers will find themselves in the news. While you can learn from

these sales, you must also be quick in listing your unique, never-to-be-forgotten item to ensure another eBay seller does not beat you to the punch and make your auction a copycat sale.

One final question, though, remains. What does eBay think of all of the notorious sales documented in the pages of this book? On the one hand, each and every one of these unusual sales generates a wave of publicity for the company. Tim Bevin, who under the eBay identity "beavisons" is one of the world's top one hundred eBay sellers and also a frequent creator of novelty items that tie into newsworthy auctions, states, "These sales keep eBay alive with talk, gossip, and create an excitement about the buying venue."

On the other hand, eBay may think this publicity takes something away from its core business, especially if the company is, as has happened in several of the most notorious sales, forced to remove an item because it violates one of the company's policies.

Whatever the case may be, eBay has remained mum on the subject although it should be known that at the company's annual convention during its tenth year in business, eBay released a limited edition set of trading cards highlighting news-making auctions. Of the ten playing cards released, only one was not included in the pages of this book. The auction? Well, that is a story for another day.

NOTES

LESSON I

6   *The story was picked up:* Candice Choi, "Businessman at Forefront of Forehead Ads," *Los Angeles Times*, January 29, 2005.

8   *Steve Westley, eBay's vice president of marketing:* From "Online Shoppers Bid Millions for Human Kidney," an article on CNN.com, September 3, 1999.

9   *On September 2, 1999, immediately:* EBay item 5568750040. Listing removed from eBay after 30-day post-auction period.

12   *The British tabloid* News of the World *paid:* BBC, "Student Sells Virginity on the Web," BBC News, world edition, March 26, 2004.

14   *She also suggested the "boyfriend":* Catherine Donaldson-

Evans, "Auction Gives New Meaning to Online Dating," Fox News, January 5, 2004.

14   *Eventually the trend got a little too hot:* Reuters, "Online Girlfriends Sell Love to Dateless," CNN, February 5, 2004.

15   *The patron stated her accoutrements were like:* "Golden Palace Has Hands Full after eBay Auction," on Golden Palace .com.

16   *Bidding was intense, but eBay pulled the auction:* "Web Suitor Bids £251,000 for Bride," BBC News, January 29, 2002.

17   *Although the man she thought had placed the bid:* Tim Richardson, "Web Wife Jilted on the Auction Block," *The Register* (UK), February 19, 2002.

LESSON II

19   *Within twelve hours of the unveiling:* Jan Disley and Nick Sommerlad, "Going for a Thong," *The Mirror* (UK), May 19, 2004.

23   *The car sold within five minutes:* Jonathan Brown, "Wife Sells DJ's Lotus on eBay in Revenge for His On-air Flirting," *The Independent* (UK), online edition, June 22, 2005.

24   *Citing as the reason for the sale:* EBay item 5527273221. Listing removed from eBay after 30-day post-auction period.

25   *It turns out she "needed some time alone":* AP, "Runaway Bride: Wedding 'Postponed,' Not Off," CNN.com, May 1, 2005, 7:04 a.m. EDT.

25   *When some eBay visitors criticized the sale:* From follow-up to item 5578195975 posted by seller malcolmmonty. Listing removed from eBay after 30-day post-auction period.

26   *For that sale, which was visited by more than 100,000 people:*

EBay item 5577585474. Listing removed from eBay after 30-day post-auction period.

30 *He sold more than 1,100 of these certificates:* Interview with seller conducted by author.

31 *"You can be an author without the drudgery"*: EBay item 2905270846, January 9, 2003.

31 *Similarly, in 2004, a German woman:* "German Girl Up for Sale on eBay," BBC News, online edition, April 20, 2004.

33 *The winning bid of $202,100:* PR newswire, Reuters, 10:05 p.m. (New York), September 9, 2004. "Lunch with Buffet Comes at a Price." San Francisco, July 15, 2004.

34 *The winner of the auction had earned multiple negative feedbacks:* From feedback left for the profile of winning bidder. EBay item 6528557289. Listing removed from eBay after 30-day post-auction period.

34 *As for the runner-up:* From eBay items 5582040073 and 6528557289. Auctions removed after 30-day post-auction period.

35 *According to the college's dean, James Larimore:* Tamar Lewin, "Online Bid Is Made, Briefly, to Save Dartmouth's Swim Team," *New York Times*, December 6, 2002.

37 *He also runs the Web site www.weddingdressguy.com:* Larry Star, "The Larry Line," *weddingdressguy.com*, July 25, 2005.

LESSON III

43 *According to Wired.com, David Ingram:* Charles Mandel, "U.S. EBay Seller Refuses Canucks," *Wired.com*, March 25, 2003.

45 *According to CNN:* Muffie Dunn, "EBay to Withdraw Diallo Shooting Item," CNN, May 2, 2001.

47   *Another item, according to* Wired Magazine: "Mir Crashes; Wreckage on eBay," Wired News, March 23, 2001.

48   *One piece of debris that was bid up to $4,500:* Ibid.

48   *According to the company, even if someone:* Troy Wolverton, "EBay Shuts Down Mir Auctions," CNET, March 23, 2001, 4:05 p.m. PST.

49   *As Linda Harrison pointed out in her column:* Linda Harrison, "U.S. Presidency Up for Grabs on eBay," *The Register* (UK), November 13, 2000, 23:18 GMT.

50   *"It's humorous, and everything like that gets blown out of proportion":* Janet Adamy, "EBay Pulls New Controversial Abercrombie & Fitch T-shirt," *Clarkson Integrator*, April 22, 2002.

55   *"Perhaps, only coincidentally," said an article in* City Beat: "EBay Exchange Still Bullish on Enron," *Houston Business Journal,* January 11, 2002.

LESSON IV

61   *In reference to the poster's sale:* "Hilton's Dog Posters for Sale on eBay," Contactmusic.com, September 7, 2004.

62   *According to the auction description:* From eBay item 3812432670. Listing removed from eBay after 30-day post-auction period.

62   *Yet at least one organization did not find the auction a laughing matter:* Kieran Crowley, "Joel's Smash Hit on eBay," *The Register* (UK), May 1, 2004.

64   *Despite his auction being canceled:* Adam Horwitz, et al., "The 101 Dumbest Moments in Business," *Business 2.0,* January/February 2004.

67   *The gum belonging to the seller:* Lindsay Kuhn, "Britney Trash Turned Treasure," eOnline, September 1, 2004.

Notes

72   *After a grueling regulation and overtime:* Adrian Harte, "Hosts Hold Their Nerve," *Euro 2004.com*, June 24, 2004.

75   *According to an article in* USA Today: "EBay Halts, Restarts Patsy Cline Wreckage Auction," *USA Today*, Tech Section, September 14, 2001.

LESSON V

87   *It is too early to tell:* GoldenPalace.com press release, "Mystifying Image of Virgin Mary on Grilled Cheese Sandwich Sold to GoldenPalace.com," November 22, 2004.

97   *Throughout the auction, eBay said:* Thomas A. Droleskey, "Missing the Real Culprit Once Again," Life Site News, April 15, 2005.

LESSON VI

107   *According to the surgeon's lawyer:* "Doctor Sells Surgery Exam Answers on eBay," AP, *USA Today*, Tech Section, May 29, 2005.

109   *The chemist further indicated:* As reported by Fox 40 News, "Pod Seller Busted on eBay." Fox took its information directly from the criminal complaint, February 4, 2003.

LESSON VI

116   *While there, Freyer and his guests:* John Freyer, *All My Life for Sale*, allmylifeforsale.com, May 12, 2005.

116   *The highest-priced item sold was a:* Ibid.

121   *Representatives of the online casino say only:* Goldenpalace

.com, "Golden Palace Pays $7,600 for Mystery Envelope." Article viewable at http://www.goldenpalaceevents.com/auctions/envelope01.php.

124 *Bidding kicked off on October 14, 2004:* "Screenwriter Clive Barker Opens Auction for Disneyland 'Haunted Mansion,' " Mouseplanet.com, "Room for 1,001?" Update for November 1–7, 2004, http://mouseplanet.com/parkupdates/dlr/dlr041101.htm. October 13, 2004.

125 *The successful suitor was:* "Room for 1,001?" Mouseplanet.com Update for week of November 1–7, 2004.

132 *Unfortunately for the seller:* Karen Schubert, "Bazaar Goes Bizarre," *USA Today*, front page of Tech Section, July 28, 2003.

LESSON VIII

137 *When asked why they did not relist:* AP, "Town Sells on eBay for $1.8 million dollars," CNN.com, December 27, 2003.

138 *The spokesperson for the governor, Amy Shuler Goodwin:* AP, "EBay Joker Auctions Off West Virginia," CNN.com, January 14, 2004, posted 1:12 p.m. EST.

140 *One DEA spokesperson was quoted:* Noah Schactman, "A Room with an Apocalyptic View," Wired.com, October 16, 2001.

141 *This service gained the establishment:* Steve Lopez, "Hold the Pickles, Please," *Time*, October 2, 2000.

LESSON IX

144 *According to the seller:* Monty Phan, "Jenny's Phone Number—from the Song—For Sale," *Miami Herald*, February 15, 2004.

Notes

145 *According to Leonard David:* Leonard David, "Personalized Moon Crash For Sale on eBay," CNN, April 9, 2004, 3:53 p.m. EDT. Originally written for Space.com.

146 *Future versions of the machines:* Jordan Legon, "For Sale: Personal Strap-on Aircraft," *CNN Technology*, January 16, 2003.

148 *Mike countered with a request for $10,000:* AP, "Microsoft Takes on Teen's Site," Microsoft.com. Found at CNN.com, January 19, 2004, 11:34 p.m. EST.

150 *"Yet the timing is perfect":* Engineers: Daniel Eisenberg, "We're For Sale, Just Click," *Time*, August 16, 1999.

151 *According to Greg Sandoval:* Greg Sandoval, "EBay Sells for $1.25 in Bogus Auction," CNET, September 24, 1999.

LESSON X

156 *All proceeds were to go to charity:* Darren Rovel, ESPN.com, February 25, 2005.

158 *After several months of trying: Court TV,* "EBay Loser Goes Literally Ballistic," CourtTV home page, May 5, 2004.

158 *According to a Poughkeepsie, New York, prosecutor:* "EBay Loser Threatened Winner's Wife with Gun," *The Inquirer* (UK), May 3, 2004.

159 *Days before he was scheduled to go to trial: Court TV,* "EBay Loser Goes Literally Ballistic," CourtTV home page, May 5, 2004.

Photo Credits

Photo Credits

© *Kalinka Cihlar*

About the Author

Christopher Cihlar was born in Northampton, Massachusetts. He holds a Ph.D. and an M.S. from Cornell University and a B.A. from Georgetown University. He was formerly employed by the not for profit that runs eBay's charity-giving function, MissionFish. He currently resides in Kensington, Maryland, with his wife, Kalinka, and their one-year-old son, Shay.